Translanguaging

Teaching English to Secondary School Students in Tanzania

Thomas R. Kagumisa

En Route Books and Media, LLC

Saint Louis, MO

⊕ *ENROUTE*
Make the time

En Route Books and Media, LLC

5705 Rhodes Avenue

St. Louis, MO 63109

Contact us at **contact@enroutebooksandmedia.com**

Cover Credit: Sebastian Mahfood

Copyright 2023 Thomas R. Kagumisa

ISBN-13: 979-8-88870-095-2

Library of Congress Control Number: 2023946706

Dedication

To my mother, Clementine Kagumisa
to whom I owe my initial stages
of first language acquisition

List of Abbreviations

CITI	Collaborative Institutional Training Initiative
Cfr.	Confer
Dr.	Doctor (a title for an eminent scholar and teacher)
EFL	English as a Foreign Language
ESL	English as a Second Language
EOP	English Only Policy
IRB	Institutional Review Board
L1	First/Native Language
L2	Second/Acquired Language
PI	Principal Investigator
Rev.	Reverend (an official title prefixed to the names of ordained Roman Catholic priests)
Sr.	Sister (a title of a Roman Catholic nun)
TL	Target Language

Table of Contents

Acknowledgments

When I first set foot on American soil from Tanzania in June 2014, I immediately realized that my ability to communicate effectively in English was limited, especially when I compared myself to native speakers. Consequently, I decided to give a leg-up to my communicative competence not only to hone my effectiveness in my job as a religious worker but also to teach the language upon returning to my home country. Hence, for the past seven years, I have been chasing after these goals. I began by earning a master's degree in English from Liberty University, Virginia, and finally, a doctoral degree in English Pedagogy from Murray State University, Kentucky. This research project was a culminating assignment of the doctoral program. I am eternally grateful to Almighty God, who has graciously inspired my efforts, especially this scholarly work from its genesis to its zenith. Doubtlessly, without His unfailing help, my educational goals would be as dead as a dodo.

Additionally, I am deeply grateful to their Excellencies: Bishop Thomas Olmsted of the Roman Catholic Diocese of Phoenix, Arizona; Bishop Desiderius Rwoma of the Roman Catholic Diocese of Bukoba, Tanzania, and his auxiliary, Bishop Method Kilaini, for giving me an opportunity to further my education while doing priestly ministry in the United States.

Special gratitude is owed to the Doctor of Arts in English Pedagogy Committee, who patiently dealt with the logistics of this project, but, in particular, to Dr. Sara Cooper, the Capstone Instructor, for the long hours spent revising, correcting, and providing helpful feedback and direction to the project. Her invaluable insights, comments, and advice have uniquely shaped this final product in a way I would never have envisioned on my own. Thanks as well to Jonathan Baskin for reviewing and granting approval to my research protocols as per Institutional Review Board (IRB) requirements.

As is common in any professional writing, peer review played a significant role in the realization of this project. In this regard, I want to recognize the assistance of dedicated colleagues: Susan Decker and Lisa Cox, who helped peer-review the project. I especially thank Judy Westley for her thorough and thoughtful suggestions that pushed me to articulate my methodology more clearly. Also, without the financial support of Mr. and Mrs. Tom Brand, it would have been difficult to cruise through the coursework and carry out the research. They selflessly scratched the bottom of their pockets to make it certain that every tuition bill that came on my table was fully covered. In the same vein, I remain ever indebted to Mr. and Mrs. Jeff Gaffney, who, aside from moral support and parental affection, generously provided me additional funding to cover the expenses associated with books and other educational resources. I have also benefited from the advice and support of many research participants, friends, and professionals, and it is difficult to reference them all here. However, at the risk of omitting some names, I must mention Rev. Solomon Bandiho, Rev. Jason Kaiza, Rev. Achilles Rwehumbiza, Rev. Gideon Rwezahura, Rev. Profilio Mulokozi, Rev. Denis Rweyunga, Sr. Dr. Hellen Bandiho, Rob Kubasco, Alexander Kashozi, Thaddeus Kagumisa, Novat Rukwago, Gift Muhando, Peter Warioba, and Daniel Oketch. To each of them, for various reasons, I am truly grateful.

Testimonials

Dr. Kagumisa addresses the complexity of the region's geography, language practices, and school system in a way only one with intimate knowledge of the region and a keen eye for cultural and linguistic nuance could do. Drawing on surveys he conducted with educators, current research, and his own experiences growing up in Tanzania's English-only system, he illuminates with loving attention important tensions among pedagogical practice, language values, and perceptions of the English Only Policy (EOP) in Tanzanian schools.

Dr. Kagumisa thus substantiates, through his own research, the recommendation that a national instructional policy allowing the use of Swahili alongside English would best support student learning and the maintenance of their cultural identities. As scholars of culturally responsive pedagogy like Gloria Ladson-Billings, Geneva Gay, and Sonia Nieto note, teaching in ways that support cultural identity are crucial to ensuring students thrive.

Sara Cooper, Ph.D.
Assistant Professor, Doctor of Arts in English Pedagogy Program
Murray State University
Murray, Kentucky, USA

Dr. Kagumisa's volume not only provides a useful overview of theories and practices of translanguaging but also models the protocols and considerations for applying translanguaging in a specific context. In doing so, Dr. Kagumisa lays out both challenges and solutions in second language instruction in a region in which a predominant language is contested to a degree. Most importantly, his work demonstrates in a significant and broadly useful way how translanguaging can, and should, be at the center of culturally sustainable second language instruction.

Kevin Binfield, Ph.D.
Professor and Director of Graduate Studies in English
Murray State University
Murray, Kentucky, USA

Learning a new language is arduous when one grows up in a multilanguage context. One component of effective communication is a natural flow, and translanguaging provides that cog that dispels clogs, and Dr. Kagumisa delineates such benefits in his research; as he discovers that translanguaging is the panacea to human labor of meaning-making incurred in the context of prevalent multilanguage cognition and transaction.

The socio-cultural implication of a potpourri of languages within a context requires an easier way to relay information quickly and to drive the cultural values and connection. Dr. Kagumisa argues that since translanguaging significantly bridges the communication gap and integrates the people of parallel socio-cultural history, it behooves our educational institutions to acknowledge its function and validate its dynamic in curriculum development.

Dr. George Ebimobowei Oti
Prosocial Pedagogy Expert
San Jacinto College
Pasadena, Texas, USA

The English-speaking world is remarkably diverse, and was imprinted throughout the twentieth century by a whirlwind of independence and decolonization movements. Language and education are at the contested center when a nation transitions to self-rule. This is the case in Tanzania, a polyglot nation where speakers of Swahili, English, and hundreds of other regional and ethnic language families regularly use different languages for different purposes. Learners in such diverse linguistic environments determine the extent to which they will make full use of *all* of their language resources, practicing translanguaging, or combining, meshing, or switching among multiple languages.

The Rev. Dr. Thomas Kagumisa reveals the complexity of translanguaging beliefs and practices in this study of Tanzanian English teachers' translanguaging beliefs and practices. These teachers experience the tension between supporting their students' right to their own languages and cultural heritages, providing students a robust background in their nation's *lingua franca*, and reconciling national education policy with the realities of the classroom. Dr. Kagumisa, who is from the Kagera region of Tanzania, supplements the insights of his research with first-hand experience.

This work has implications for educators in any linguistically-diverse place (including the United States) where teachers must understand their own translanguaging beliefs and advocate for the policies and resources necessary to serve their students.

Dr. Zachary Garrett
Assistant Professor of English
Murray State University
Murray, Kentucky, USA

Dr. Kagumisa's study offers great promise for the reform of English instruction in Tanzania and, by extension, throughout the world, and the methods discussed will be helpful to any country struggling with a need for language acquisition in order to participate in a global linguistic system, such as Cameroonian students learning French, Uzbek students learning Russian, and Basque students learning Spanish, to name some examples. In short, Dr. Kagumisa provides a generally useful study on a method of language acquisition in an increasingly interconnected world.

Dr. Sebastian Mahfood, OP
Returned Peace Corps Volunteer, Tunisia (1994-1996)
Retired Professor of Interdisciplinary and Intercultural Studies
St. Louis, Missouri, USA

Foreword

If there is one thing I know about education after many years in the classroom, working with graduate students, and directing a federally-funded education program, it is this: context is everything. Or, as a student recently pointed out, the answer to any pedagogical question is usually, "it depends." Contrary to the trend in education scholarship of identifying and celebrating "best practices," the only best practices I have encountered are those specific to a place, a moment, a group of students, and a sociocultural context. This is part of what makes Kagumisa's work essential. As he points out in this comprehensive analysis and discussion of English instruction in Tanzanian secondary school classrooms, we know that translanguaging is an effective pedagogical practice. What we didn't know before this volume is how it might be effective in Tanzania, a country where, among its many unique characteristics, the average citizen speaks three languages: Swahili, English, and one of more than 120 indigenous languages. Kagumisa addresses the complexity of the region's geography, language practices, and school system in a way only one with intimate knowledge of the region and a keen eye for cultural and linguistic nuance could do. Drawing on surveys he conducted with educators, current research, and his own experiences growing up in Tanzania's English-only system, he illuminates with loving attention important tensions among pedagogical practice, language values, and perceptions of the English Only Policy (EOP) in Tanzanian schools.

Kagumisa's survey respondents represent three Tanzanian regions, including the two biggest cities (Dar es Salaam and Mwanza) and his own native region (Kagera). He blends data on educators' attitudes and beliefs about translanguaging with a rich discussion of the history of monolingualism in Tanzanian schools, the value of translanguaging and, significantly, specific recommendations for moving forward. While scholarly projects often stake claim in the realm of either theory or practice, it is through the marriage of the two that the possibility for change arises. Kagumisa achieves this union, attending thoughtfully to both theories of language acquisition and matters of policy and teaching methods. He cites García and Leiva (2014) who remind us that one aim of translanguaging is movement toward social justice. By helping us to understand existing attitudes, beliefs, and practices of Tanzanian educators, he elucidates what is possible on the ground, in the schools, for actual students. He substantiates, through his own research, the recommendation that a national instructional policy allowing the use of Swahili alongside English would best support student learning and the maintenance of their cultural identities. As scholars of culturally responsive pedagogy like Gloria Ladson-Billings, Geneva Gay, and Sonia Nieto note, teaching in ways that support cultural identity are crucial to ensuring students thrive.

I had the pleasure of reading early drafts of this work as the advisor to Kagumisa's doctoral capstone project at Murray State University. In my notes to nearly every draft, I encouraged him to seek publication. His work is not only expertly rendered, but fills a gap in scholarship, improving our understanding of the inextricable link between local and global conversations about translanguaging.

Getting to know Kagumisa over the course of our many meetings, I learned that he is not only an exceptional scholar, but a kind and thoughtful person, one guided by faith and a desire to make the world better. We had many conversations about his experiences in Phoenix, AZ, my home town, where he serves as a Catholic priest and has no doubt touched many lives. The best scholarly work is born of a meeting of the head and the heart. This work would not be so impactful were it not driven by compassion. Taken up, the ideas here are capable of significantly shifting the landscape of Tanzanian education.

Sara Cooper, Ph.D.
Assistant Professor,
Doctor of Arts in English Pedagogy Program
Department of English and Philosophy
Murray State University

Chapter 1

General Introduction

Unlike the rest of the former British colonies, Tanzania chose to espouse Swahili as a language of instruction in public primary schools. The motive was to achieve national cohesion in a country of more than 120 constitutive tribes—each with its own indigenous language, traditions, and customs. Thus, in 1965, the Ministry of Education and Culture decreed that

> The medium of instruction in primary schools shall be Swahili, and English shall be a compulsory subject. ... The medium of instruction in secondary school education shall continue to be English except for the teaching of other approved languages, and Swahili shall be a compulsory subject up to the Ordinary Level. (Ngonyani, n.d., pp. 39-45).

In line with this policy, English is only introduced as a compulsory subject during the third of the 7-year primary educational program (see Appendix A: School Systems—Tanzania Vs American). However, students hardly speak the language—let alone write it—by the time they graduate from primary education. Despite the lack of proficiency, English becomes the medium of instruction as students transition from primary to secondary school. Educational policymakers assume that by repeated exposure to the language at the secondary school level, students will learn grammar inductively

1

and be functional bilinguals at the zenith of their secondary education program. Thus, monolingual instructional strategies plus other ancillary techniques such as imposing different forms of punishments to those who violate the language policy, posting placards with words "Speak English," "English Only," and "English Zone" on school facilities—to name no more—have been enforced to help students break through their linguistic barriers. Yet, again, students graduate from the secondary school program with limited communicative competence in English, notwithstanding the efforts discussed above. Consequently, students' limited competence in English affects their performance in other subject areas.

The fact often overlooked is that the Ministry of Education's language policy endorses the *late immersion mode* of content-based learning in which students are not fully exposed to the English language until the end of primary school or the beginning of the secondary school program. Unfortunately, this model has proven ineffective in many cases. The results would have been different if the *early total immersion mode* had been implemented in all academic instruction from kindergarten through high school. This assumption was backed up by Denham and Lobeck (2013), whose study confirmed that learning a second language is easier the younger you are and becomes more challenging after you grow up. Hence, the best time to learn English, also known as *the critical period for second language acquisition*, would be from kindergarten through primary seven, when students transition from early childhood to puberty.

Another strategy that will help students acquire English skills is translanguaging. Translanguaging literally means the practice of alternating between languages (in this case, English and Swahili) to maximize students' learning of the content as well as the acquisition of English skills. Despite being discouraged by the education system in Tanzania, some teachers have been applying translanguaging strategies for the very purpose mentioned above. Previous studies conducted globally have confirmed that when students are allowed to use alternative languages as resources in subject-related learning situations, they are able to develop conceptual knowledge to a greater extent than students who are not offered this opportunity. Therefore, to ascertain whether translanguaging would be an effective strategy in the Tanzanian context, the Principal Investigator (henceforth PI) conducted an exploratory survey of English educators' perspectives and beliefs on the strategy. The results of the survey served as a basis for making appropriate recommendations. The ultimate goal was to seek to try other instructional methods and depart from the monolingual and/or content-based models since they have proven ineffective.

However, the legitimate question that was carefully considered was whether the translanguaging policy would work in a multilingual country like Tanzania. As noted previously, the 120 tribes of Tanzania speak more than 112 indigenous languages, most of which are not mutually intelligible. The number of speakers for each language ranges between a few thousand and millions. In general, the average educated Tanzanian speaks three languages: a) indigenous language at home and local communities, b) Swahili as a national language, and c) English for international communication. According to Ngonyani (n.d.), only 10 percent of the Tanzania population speak Swahili as their native language; 90 percent speak

Swahili, and at least one indigenous language, and 15 percent speak English, Swahili, and at least one indigenous language. Graph 1 below demonstrates the linguistic distribution of the Tanzanian population.

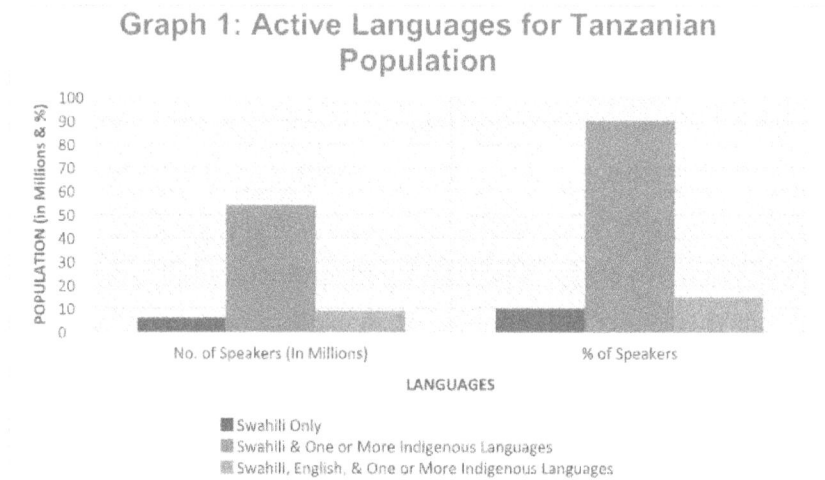

Graph 1: Active Languages for Tanzanian Population

As can be seen from the graph, the majority of the population speaks Swahili (and at least one indigenous language). Therefore, if translanguaging strategies were to be adapted, it would be between English and Swahili.

Research Questions

The central question that drove the exploration of the phenomenon described above was: *What are Tanzanian educators' core beliefs and perspectives related to the effectiveness of translanguaging strategies in teaching English as a Foreign Language (EFL) to secondary school students?* However, to narrow the focus of the study, that broad question was split into seven more sub-questions, namely:

1. Do you apply translanguaging methods in your English class? If your answer is affirmative, explain the manner and the extent to which you practice the strategies.
2. What are your core beliefs, suggestions, and perspectives with regard to the effectiveness of translanguaging practices?
3. How do students respond to the incorporation of other languages in the EFL lesson?
4. What are your beliefs and perspectives on the English Only Policy?
5. What socio-cultural beliefs do people associate with translanguaging strategies?
6. Might students use the translanguaging approach at the same time manage to think in the target language (English) with minimal interference from their native language(s)?
7. What translanguaging methods can we use to effect teaching and learning English as a Foreign Language (EFL)?

Purpose and Significance of the Study

The purpose of this study was to explore English educators' beliefs and perspectives on the effectiveness of translanguaging strategies in teaching English as a Foreign Language to secondary school students in Tanzania. As noted earlier, this study was important because the monolingual instructional policy, which has been in place for decades, has failed students in many educational aspects. Hence, it is time educational policymakers considered authorizing alternative instructional methods, including translanguaging. But how could they know that translanguaging would be effective in the Tanzanian context unless we ascertained its efficacy from the educators who are actively engaged in teaching, and have also been applying the strategy (albeit contrary to the existing monolingual policy)? For that reason, the current study was but necessary.

The positive outcome of the study would benefit stakeholders of education in various ways. First, the researcher assumed that once exposed to the effectiveness of translanguaging, educators and educational policymakers would be prompted to embrace the method freely and, therefore, enhance students' sense of pride, multilingual heritage, culture, and identity the monolingual approach would have otherwise suppressed. Second, educators would consider espousing translanguaging as a viable and effective alternative for teaching English instead of exclusively relying on monolingual instructional strategies. Consequently, the translanguaging approach would foster students' linguistic development, especially those with limited English skills, by promoting interpretative discussions and translating languages in various contexts outside the classroom (Cummins, 2007). Third, the study would help English educators discover the need to use translanguaging to equip students with a broader range of linguistic tools, communicative sensitivity, and cognitive skills that come with multilingual ability (Denham and Lobeck, 2013).

Definition of Terms

The following is a brief description of terms that the reader will need in order to understand the content of the study. Important to realize is that these terms are contrasted with the words of everyday language in the interest of precision.

Translanguaging

Translanguaging is a relatively new term that has appeared with growing frequency in research about the education of bilingual or multilingual students. Consequently, different scholars have come up with various definitions of translanguaging, some of which also lack consistency. However, Poza (2017), in his article, "Translanguaging: Definitions, Implications, and Further Needs in Burgeoning Inquiry," offers a somewhat comprehensive and reliable definition of the term. After critically analyzing 53 scholarly articles on the phenomenon, he deducted three categories of translanguaging:

a) *Language Alteration*: "Translanguaging refers to the combination of two or more languages in a systematic way within the same learning activity" (Cenoz & Gorter, 2011, p. 359). It is also a skill that happens naturally in everyday life whereby the speaker or writer receives information in one language and uses it or applies it in the other language (Williams, 2002).

b) *Heterogrossic Views Tied to Sociocultural Theories*: Translanguaging is a practice of using both languages in a dynamically and functionally integrated manner to organize and mediate mental processes in understanding, speaking, literacy, and, not least, learning (Lewis, Jones, & Baker, 2012).

c) *Heterogrossic Views with Schooling and Societal Implications*: "Translanguaging is related to other fluid language practices that scholars have called by different names... [B]ut what makes translanguaging different from these other fluid practices is that it is transformative, attempting to wipe out hierarchy...Thus, translanguaging could be a mechanism for social justice, especially when teaching students from language minoritized communities" (García & Leiva, 2014, p. 200).

Hence, these three categories will serve as working definitions throughout this project. However, we shall limit their use to schooling and sociocultural learning environment, thereby eliminating societal implications.

Codeswitching

The majority of scholars define codeswitching as the use of more than one language in a single communicative episode or a practice in a discourse to signal changes in context by using alternate grammatical systems or subsystems or codes (Nilep, 2017; Heller, 1988). The word language as used here implies lexical items, syntactic/morphological constructions, or prosodic phenomena. Accordingly, scholars distinguish between two main types of codeswitching:

a) *Intersentential Codeswitching*: one that occurs between clauses or sentences whereby each clause or sentence is in a different language.

b) *Intrasentential Codeswitching*: one that occurs within the same clause, word, or at the morpheme level (see examples in the "Translanguaging Strategies" section of this project).

Translanguaging Vs. Codeswitching

The key point to note is that translanguaging is not the same as codeswitching. Translanguaging is more than codeswitching and usually occurs from the sentence level to the discourse level. Celic and Seltzer (2013) specified that translanguaging has nothing to do with switching between codes at the word, syntactic, or morphemic level (intrasentential codeswitching). Notably, then, the only type of codeswitching tied to translanguaging is intersentential code-switching since, in this linguistic practice, the speaker alternates between languages at the sentence level. Thus, regarding this study, the term translanguaging will partly connote intersentential codeswitching.

Code Meshing

Another terminology that is gaining wide usage in modern sociolinguistic discourse is code meshing. In fact, code meshing is preferred to code-switching due to the practice of using broad rhetorical strategies, structural units, and a full continuum of bilingualism, which are specific characteristics of code meshing. According to Michael-Luna and Canagarajah (2007), code meshing is "A communicative device used for specific rhetorical and ideological purposes in which a multilingual speaker intentionally integrates local and academic discourse as a form of resistance, reappropriation, and/or transformation of the academic discourse" (p. 56). In other words, code meshing means a "social practice which intentionally integrates local and academic discourse in order to index specific discursive, ideological, and rhetorical stances of the interlocutor" (Michael-Luna & Canagarajah, 2007, p. 57). Markedly, code meshing and translanguaging share plenty of similarities and, ipso facto, the PI will use them interchangeably to mean the same.

Monolingualism (English Only Policy)

As an instructional strategy, monolingualism or English Only Policy (EOP) refers to "the assumptions that: a) the target language (TL) should be used exclusively for instructional purposes without recourse to students' first language (L1); (b) translation between L1 and TL has no place in the language classroom; and (c) within immersion and bilingual programs, the two languages should be kept rigidly separate" (Cummins, 2007, p. 221).

Bilingualism/Multilingualism

In the context of this research, bilingualism or multilingualism simply means the use of two or more languages during classroom instruction, in which case one can rightly speak of translanguaging.

Chapter 2

Literature Review

The aim of this literature review is to discuss the results of other studies that are closely related to our topic, to bring to the fore the ongoing dialogue about the topic, to identify the gap in the previous studies, and point out how the current study will attempt to fill in the existing gap. Additionally, the literature is hereby used to assess how our topic is informed by and connected to the work of others. While going about this process, the PI did not only summarize the work of others but evaluated them, pointed out deficiencies, and determined how they contradict or align with the topic under study. In essence, the PI attempted to situate the topic of inquiry within a large pre-existing knowledge that is captured in such things as books, journal articles, newspaper articles, conference papers, and websites (Dana & Yendol-Hoppey, 2014). Correspondingly, the literature was organized according to research sub-questions to help the reader understand how the proposed study adds to and abridges the research already completed (Creswell & Creswell, 2018).

English Only: Current Policy of Instruction in Tanzania

As discussed previously, English has been the medium of instruction in all Tanzanian public secondary schools since 1965. The assumption is that when students are instructed in English Only classrooms, they can think in that language with minimal interference from their native languages or Swahili. That ability affords them a proficiency in English once they have mastered the language. A similar belief maintains that when a non-native speaker teaches English to second language learners, the monolingual approach challenges and encourages both the teacher and the learner to communicate in English in a formal and informal settings— hence, an opportunity to practice and master the language. This idea was backed up by Ekawati and Setyarini (2014) in their article, "Students' Attitude toward Monolingual Approach in English Classes at Smalab Salatiga." Accordingly, the article investigated students' attitudes toward a monolingual approach to teaching English as a foreign language. The study results indicated students' reasonably positive attitude toward the EOP [English Only Policy] as well as their optimism in acquiring English proficiency. Additionally, the study claimed that the EOP "makes the language [English] real and develops learners' in-built language system … [because] successful L2 learning involves the separation and distinction of L1 and L2. [Therefore] students should be shown the importance of L2 through its continual use" (Ekawati & Setyarini, 2014, n.p).

Ekawati and Setyarini's (2014) study connects to Pardede (2013), who argued that overusing L1 makes students believe that word for word translation is a helpful technique and may be tempted to transfer L1 meaning into L2, which may not always be appropriate. However, despite the monolingual policy's ability to provide students with more exposure to English and more chances of acquiring it, the studies cited above neglect that the EOP kills students' L1 and deprives them of social, cultural, and linguistic benefits that are tied to multilingual ability. That is why Van Lier

(2008) recommended an ecological approach to language teaching, that is, developing a new language alongside the existing one.

Another belief in which Tanzania's monolingual instructional policy is founded is that maximizing the amount of time spent on the target language improves learning efficiency and that the use of students' L1 impedes the acquisition of L2. In line with this contention, Hoang, Jan, and Yang (2010), in their study: *English Only Classrooms: Ideology Versus Reality*, set out to investigate the extent to which students understand and participate in English-only classrooms. Their study concluded that using "EOP with low desirability and effectiveness does not always facilitate learning a language as many have claimed. [The] policy appears to interfere with learning when it hinders thorough comprehension, prevents full participation, and creates a psychological blockage" (p. 9). In the same vein, Pacher and Field's (2001) study maintained that no evidence could be found to assert that teaching in L2 has a direct causal connection with more effective learning of the target language. In reality, Hong, Jan, and Yang's contention sound true since the insistence of EOP excludes struggling students from participating fully in learning, thereby leading to incomprehension and perhaps resentment. Additionally, as Miles (2004) remarked, many English teachers in Tanzania are non-native speakers and, therefore, the EOP may, and certainly does, impede their ability to communicate effectively with students, compromising their ability to teach.

Tanzania's monolingual approach towards teaching English is directly linked to the *Direct Method*. As described by Celce-Murcia, Brinton, and Snow (2014) in their textbook: *Teaching English as a Second Language or Foreign Language*, the direct method stresses the exclusive use of the target language in the classroom, and it is founded on five tenets: (a) No use of the mother tongue is permitted; (b) Actions and pictures are used to make meaning clear; (c) Grammar is learned inductively through repeated exposure to language in use, not through rules about forms; (d) Literary texts are used for pleasure and are not analyzed grammatically; and (e) The teacher must be a native speaker or have native-like proficiency in the target language. Among the protagonists of the direct method was Krashen (1985), cited in Hoang, Jan, and Yang (2010), who stated, "The ESL/EFL classroom medium should be in English because of the significant relationship between comprehensible input in L2 and proficiency, and availability of the target language environment is of paramount importance to success in a new language" (p. 13). However, notwithstanding the rational arguments about the direct method, it would still prove ineffective in a Tanzanian context since most English educators in the country are struggling with what the authors call a *native-like proficiency* in English. Also, as mentioned previously, the exclusive use of the target language in the classroom inhibits students' comprehension of the lesson, let alone the suppression of their L1.

Effectiveness of Translanguaging Strategies

Although the translanguaging approach has always been criticized by the protagonists of the monolingual policy, the recent study confirms its efficacy in various contexts. Therefore, we can only anticipate that the same approach may prove effective in the Tanzanian context. Garcia and Kano's (2014) article: "Translanguaging as Process and Pedagogy: Developing the English Writing of Japanese Students in the US," which features as chapter 11 in Conteh and Meier's editorial work, is one of the recent scholarly works that present facts about the efficacy of translanguaging strategies. The article seeks to establish an instructional space where translanguaging can be used to develop bilingual students' academic writing in English. It also seeks to identify the advantages of translanguaging pedagogy for both bilingual and monolingual learners and the difficulties in enacting the translanguaging strategies. Since the purpose of our project is to explore whether translanguaging can help Tanzanian secondary school students acquire necessary English skills and, if so, how this pedagogical method can be applied to achieve educational goals, then Garcia and Kano's scholarship fits well in the context of our topic. The two authors maintain that although the lesson's goal is to produce English proficiency in L2 learners, it cannot be achieved without working with and through students' L1. They also argue that when students are allowed to express themselves in L1, they develop their thinking in that same language, and when that development of thinking is not conditioned to occur in L2, they can write well in L2 once they develop proficiency in it. In fact, the authors point out that,

> In a translanguaging classroom, by rejecting the subjugation of one language to the other and giving agency to bilingual students to self-regulate their language practices in learning, diverse linguistic and cultural repertoires are harnessed to their fullest extent. Through these experiences, bilingual students can construct truly bilingual identities and enrich their lan-

guage and academic experiences... What are needed in the 21ˢᵗ century are more classroom spaces where translanguaging is not seen as an illegitimate practice, or solely understood as scaffold for those learning a new language, but a resource for all students to learn and be part of the dynamic multilingual turn. (Garcia & Kano, 2014, p. 275)

Garcia and Kano's scholarship aligns with Creese and Black-ledge's (2010) scholarship on "Translanguaging in the Bilingual Classroom"—a process that helps students negotiate their multilingual and multicultural identities. They also reference Al Tale and Alqahtani's (2012) scholarship on "Code-meshing Versus Target-Language Only for EFL" and how code-meshing facilitates language sustenance for beginner students. Additionally, the article connects to Hornberger and Link's (2012) approach of allowing students to draw from across all their existing language skills rather than restricting them within monolingual instructional assumptions. However, the article does not address the cultural benefits of translanguaging, nor does it provide adequate options about translanguaging methods and resources.

Besides Garcia and Kano's scholarship, several other authorships have endeavored to demonstrate the effectiveness of translanguaging and/or the use of multiple languages in teaching English. For instance, in their popular textbook: *Linguistics for Everyone: An Introduction*, Denham and Lobeck (2013) argued that discouraging multilinguistic students from using their native languages in class deprives them of manifold benefits. They maintained that being multilingual gives students a wider range of

linguistic tools at their disposal, equips them with superior communicative sensitivity, and empowers them with cognitive skills as
opposed to their monolingual counterparts. Denham and Lobeck's
ideas are trustworthy because their textbook carefully examines
how language varies from country to country, region to region, and
city to city; they discuss what is true about language and what is
not; they explore multiple ideas about language that are rooted in
social and cultural (mis)perceptions. Since Tanzania has a multilingual and multicultural population, Denham and Lobeck's editorial work could be a valuable resource for the topic under study.
Additionally, the editors address the popular misconception about
multilingualism that bilingual speakers can't keep the two languages they speak straight. Their findings prove that "[b]ilingual
children possess a number of cognitive advantages over monolingual peers" (Denham & Lobeck, 2013, pp. 48).

In support of Denham and Lobeck is the scholarship of Auerbach (1993) that contradicts the belief that using L1 impedes progress in English acquisition. His study revealed that translanguaging between L1 and L2 reduces practical barriers to English acquisition and allows for more rapid progress in English. Also, with
translanguaging, students with a limited background of literacy and
schooling feel empowered and become successful. The experience
of a Saudi Ph.D. student who was enrolled in a linguistic program
in the U.S. sheds more light on this phenomenon. When she en-
tered an English classroom in her home country,

She began to address the undergraduate students in English,
only to have them stop her and say in Arabic, "No, we don't

know what you're saying [...] we don't know English. Tell us in Arabic so we can understand." Her surprised action was to think, "This is my first-time teaching [...] I'm not going to ruin it for myself [...] I'm gonna follow the rules." Her coworker told her, "Don't listen to them [...] that's the school policy [...] you have to speak in English all the time." [Finally], she decided that she had no choice but to use Arabic despite the policy. "The result," she recalls, "was immediate: they were responsive [...] they were actively engaged." (Brutt-Griffler, 2017, n.p.)

The above experience purportedly asserts that if teaching English in a multilingual classroom in a country like Tanzania is to succeed, it must adapt to the presence of multiple languages (in this case, Swahili).

Another legitimate concern about the use of Swahili in learning English is that students are likely to think in Swahili as they speak English. This would consequently affect their proficiency in English. Nevertheless, there is enough evidence to support the claim that since students do not start by thinking in English, allowing for the exploration of ideas in Swahili supports a gradual, developmental process in which the use of the Swahili language drops off naturally as it becomes less necessary (Auerbach, 1993). Thus, enforcing the English Only Policy is tantamount to neglecting the fact that a Tanzanian student's thinking, feeling, and artistic life are very much rooted in Swahili and their mother tongues. Notably, Auerbach's study answers sub-question six of this inquiry as to whether students might use the translanguaging approach and manage to think in the target language (English) with minimal interference from their native languages.

To summarize the effectiveness of Translanguaging in English acquisition, one can appeal to the words of Piasecka (1988), who contended:

> They [native languages] show that [their] use reduce[s] anxiety and enhance[s] the effective environment of learning; take[s] into account sociocultural factors; facilitate[s] incorporation of leaners' life experiences; and allow[s] for learner-centered curriculum development. (p. 18)

Students' Attitudes Toward Translanguaging

The current trend in education is to focus on the needs and concerns of individual students—hence, the *learner-centered ideology*. Imposing an instructional method at odds with students' interests is always met with resentment and repudiation. Therefore, before we attempt to propose a translanguaging method to Tanzanian students, it is worthwhile to survey students' reactions to the same method in other contexts.

In her article, "Codeswitching as a Strategy Use[*sic*] in an EFL Classroom," Pei-shi (2012) intended to examine the use of codeswitching in an English classroom and to investigate if L1 is necessary for English learning processes. Among other outcomes, the researcher discovered that students indicated a desire to have a teacher use L1 for an average of 20% of the lesson time. Furthermore, they considered the alternation between their L1 and English a helpful technique toward achieving better comprehension. They also believed that "[t]he use of code-meshing helped them understand difficult concepts [they] faced in their learning" (Pei-shi, 2012, p.1674). These findings correspond to Ahmad and Jusoff's (2009) arguments quoted by Pei-shi (2012) that translanguaging between students' L1 and the TL helps students understand new vocabulary, recognize complex concepts, and know how to use grammar rules appropriately. Hence, we can rightly assume that once translanguaging policy is adapted to the Tanzanian contexts, students would embrace it with contentment, and subsequently, make the most of it.

Similarly, Al-Nofaie's (2010) research entitled "[t]he Attitude of Teachers and Students towards Using Arabic in EFL Classrooms in Saudi-Public Schools—A Case Study" confirmed students' positive attitudes toward using L1 in learning English. The purpose of the study was to investigate students' attitudes on the topic in Saudi Intermediate School for female students. After gathering and analyzing data from 30 students and three teachers through interviews, questionnaires, and observation protocols, the author concluded that "[t]he majority of students were in favor of the systematic use of Arabic, and they expressed their desire to practice the new language. . . . They did not ignore the feeling of comfort that Arabic can create, especially when used for certain purposes" (p. 78). Al-Nofaie's findings correspond to Tien and Liu (2012), who found out that low proficiency students in Taiwanese EFL classes considered the alternate use between their mother tongue and English a helpful technique towards achieving better comprehension, especially when providing equivalents and giving classroom procedures. Also, the same scholarly work connects to Burden (2000), whose study concluded that the occasional use of L1 in an English class as a means of relaxing students was welcomed by the majority of students. However, if upon being introduced to the translanguaging policy Tanzanian students exhibit similar positive attitudes, care should be taken as to which language dominates the classroom instruction. While the use of Swahili may create an atmosphere conducive to proper learning, it may limit students' exposure to English if overused, and, consequently, deter their acquisition of English.

Several other studies have described students' responses and reactions toward the use of translanguaging in a multilingual classroom. For instance, in "Differential Performance by English Language Learners on an Inquiry-based Science Assessment," Turkan and Liu (2012) argued that if students do not have necessary skills in the language of instruction, they often have problems obtaining access to the lesson content. Consequently, they are precluded from demonstrating the full repertoire of the content knowledge they have. Moreover, as a result of the language barrier, "Students suffer the lack of motivation, interest, and knowledge development" (Turkan & Liu, 2012, n.p.). However, the purpose of Turkan and Liu's study was to investigate how a translanguaging primary science classroom in which teachers and students are enabled to use all available language resources may benefit science learning. Nevertheless, the study attests that translanguaging strategies can be effective not only in English lessons but also in science subjects.

Socio-cultural Beliefs and Facts Concerning Translanguaging

Although the common beliefs about monolingualism are that using English only during instruction maximizes learners' chances to acquire the language, inculcates a sense of pride among learners, and reflects the teacher's linguistic competence, research has proven the opposite. Denham & Lobeck, (2013) confirmed that children who are forbidden to speak their heritage language at school could lose self-esteem and may come to think of the language of their parents and family as bad or stupid. They also affirmed that alternating between English and other languages is not a sign of a lack of proficiency in English but linguistic expertise. Precisely,

> Being able to code-switch requires a great deal of linguistic and conversational expertise. . . . A Spanish-English bilingual, for example, may use an English word or phrase because it has a meaning a Spanish word doesn't, or he or she may switch from Spanish to English (or vice versa) because of the social context. For example, codeswitching may depend on who is being spoken to, what is being talked about, and when the conversation is taking place. (Denham & Lobeck, 2013, p. 49)

Vladimirovna, Sergreevna, and Vladislavovna's (2020) study: "Cultural Impact of Codeswitching on Modern Bilingualism" provides additional facts on the socio-cultural benefits of translanguaging. The purpose of the study was to investigate the cultural influence of codeswitching on the language of modern-day bilinguals. Appropriately, the authors observed 157 students at the American University of Sharjah who speak different languages, including English, Arabic, and Urdu. The study showed that "Bilingual students, who switch from language to language, are prone to language creativity in speech more often than other students; thus, they are more successful in studying other subjects" (n.p.). In other words, this study confirms Denham and Lobeck's (2013) findings. In light of these studies, one may rightly assume that the use of English alongside Swahili during classroom instruction will not only enhance language creativity among Tanzania students but also augment their success in other subject areas.

According to Nakayama and Halualani (2010), the extended meaning of translanguaging involves changing from one way of speaking to another between or within interactions and includes changes in accent, dialect, or language. In particular, translanguaging between different accents as manifested by cross-cultural individuals can imply stereotypes or changes of perceptions. For instance, "In the United States, people who have a Southern accent are perceived as being less intelligent and having a lower socioeconomic status when compared to individuals with a standard American accent" (Wothry, n.d., n.p.). Thus, when people become conscious of the unfavorable impression that results from their accent, they can make an effort to improve on their way of speaking, and finally, be able to switch quickly between their native accent when speaking with friends and family, and their modified accent when speaking in professional settings. A similar phenomenon can be reflected in the Tanzanian context concerning English and Swahili usage. Petzell (2012) noted that English and Swahili have separate roles in society, and it is not contradictory to think highly of both languages since they have different domains. However, English is priced in various domains such as technological modernism, external ideals, and above all, it is perceived as a magical key to social prestige and power. Therefore, those who speak the language with high proficiency levels are always held in high esteem.

Although Swahili remains an indispensable medium of communication in the public sector, English is viewed as a means of obtaining good-paying jobs in the modern sector and is associated with elitism (higher education, private business, globalized segments of society's landscape, etc.). The implication of this sociocultural phenomenon is obvious: since English is learned in a predominantly Swahili environment—with students interacting on a daily basis with families, playmates, local businesses, etc., in Swahili—the effective learning of English dictates the use of translanguaging strategies between the two languages. In this way, English learning will focus on the actual language use and amplify communicative creativity that arises from the coexistence between English and Swahili (Bwenge, 2012).

Translanguaging Techniques

We cannot talk about the efficacy of translanguaging without exploring translanguaging techniques that are effective from a practical standpoint. Although a considerable amount of research has been accomplished in this particular field, care has to be taken to identify what specific techniques may prove profitable to students in a Tanzanian context.

Intersentential Translanguaging

A typical analysis of translanguaging techniques is found in Wibowo, Yuniasih, and Neelfianti's (2017) scholarly article: "Analysis of Types of Codeswitching and Code Mixing by the Sixth President of the Republic of Indonesia's Speech at the National of Independence Day[*sic*]." The article aimed to describe the types of codeswitching and codemixing in the spoken language. Despite the grammatical and syntactical flaws that characterize the article, the content provides valuable, relevant information to our topic. The authors identify two significant strategies of translanguaging: *intersentential translanguaging* and *intrasentential translanguaging.* Intersentential translanguaging occurs when the speaker alternates between clauses and sentences of different languages in the same speech. For example, the following excerpt from a secondary school English lesson in Jaffna, Sri Lanka, illustrates how translanguaging between English and Tamil is done intersententially:

Teacher: We will practice question forms next. (to pupil 1): **Ninkaal vaankoo** (*You come*) [Pupil comes forward and teacher gives her a picture to hold]

Teacher (speaking to class): - Card, **iva inta paTattuaal enTu yosiyunkoo.** (*Okay, imagine that she is the person depicted in the picture*)

Teacher (speaking to pupil 2: - **Ini niir ummuTaya keeLvikalay vaasiyum.** (*Now, you read your questions*)

Pupil 2: Who are you?

Pupil 1: I am a policeman.

Teacher: Write down complete answers for these questions. (writes questions on board in English).

Pupil: Miss, board-**ilai irukkiratayum eLutirattaa**? *(Miss, should we also write what's on the board?)*. (Ferguson, 2003, p.5)

This way of translanguaging provides access to English medium texts and helps students with limited proficiency scaffold knowledge construction. It might also prove effective if applied to secondary school students in Tanzania.

Intrasentential Translanguaging

Intrasentential, also known as *an insertional method*, occurs at the word level or can involve longer phrases or several words and even sentences (Denham and Lobeck, 2013). Blommaert (1997) provided some examples of utterances from campus Swahili which he described as mixing standard varieties of both Swahili and English into a pattern that is systematically and pragmatically coherent:

Sasa hivi wana …wanaanza kuamini ….lakini sasa haija**pickup** … haija**pick**… ni hali ambayo kwa kweli **it is still deteriorating** … lakini kwenye **situation** kama hiyo hata kama umepata nafasi ya kusoma nafikiri **it's just low… they can't go on ….**

[*Right now they ... they start to believe .... But now it hasn't picked up yet, it hasn't picked .... It is a situation which really is still deteriorating. But in a situation like this, even if you got the opportunity to study, I think it's low, they can't go on....*] (Bwenge, 2017, p. 179)

Despite its ability to convey the message in what appears to be a communicative innovation, intrasentential translanguaging may not be ideal for the Tanzanian context. As can be predicted, intrasentential translanguaging can result in a distinctly new Swahili-English mixed language. In fact, as observed by Abdulaziz-Mkilifi (1972), with this type of translanguaging, it is very likely that a new spoken language in the form of Swahili-English dialect or variety will emerge in Tanzania. On the contrary, by proposing translanguaging as a feasible instructional strategy, we do not intend to create a new language or dialect but to facilitate students' acquisition of English skills while at the same time sustaining their proficiency in Swahili.

The more compelling strategies of translanguaging are found in Celic and Seltzer's (2013) book: *Translanguaging: A Cuny-Nysieb Guide for Educators*. The book was developed by CUNY-NYSIED, the collaborative project of the Research Institute for the Study of Language in Urban Society (RISLUS) and the Ph.D. program in Urban Education at the Graduate Center, New York. The purpose of the book was to provide practical assistance on how to use translanguaging to help facilitate more effective learning of content and language by bilingual students. From this book, we select some strategies that may sound relevant to secondary school classrooms in Tanzania.

Multilingual Learning Environment

By this strategy, the authors suggest that the school landscape should make bilingual students' languages visible to the school community and build students' awareness of their classmates' languages. This would mean that all signboards and public information on the notice board should be written in English with the parallel translation in students' L1. Also, all announcements can be made in both languages.

Integrated Instruction

"Integrated Instruction involves finding meaningful ways to develop language and literacy abilities and content learning over an extended period of time" (Celic & Seltzer, 2013, p. 50). Thus, learning about a topic through English and students' L1 over an extended period can help students develop a deeper understanding of the content. Also, according to the authors, when students are given opportunities to speak, read, and write about a content area topic in both English and their L1, they develop linguistic skills for academic purposes.

Multilingual Writing Partners

In this strategy, the teacher pairs students strategically so they can help each other grow as writers in both English and their home languages. "As they have a multilingual conversation about the text they are writing, students use academic language, hone their listening skills, and talk about text and language in a way that is authentic" (Celic & Seltzer, 2013, p. 71). Accordingly, the teacher can: (a) allow students brainstorm ideas about the topic in their L1 and then write in English; (b) have students jointly construct a piece of writing in English and then discuss, negotiate, and give suggestions in L1 (the resulting product is a piece of writing in English informed and improved by students' negotiation in L1); (c) read a partner's writing in English then discuss revisions and edits in L1.

Using Multilingual Texts

Research shows that bilingual students benefit from reading texts in English and their home language. Thus, using texts in L1 can help students build background knowledge about a text, whether it is an informational text or a piece of literature. Celic & Seltzer (2013) argued that this background knowledge improves students' comprehension while reading the related text in English, and it is a powerful scaffold that all teachers can take advantage of. Also, as they read multilingual texts, students learn important academic content, strengthen their languages, and develop their bilingualism and bilingual identities. The best ways to achieve these goals is to: use an English text but conduct a class in students' L1 to discuss and analyze the content of the text; choose texts that have a multilingual version or create translations of an existing English text; supplement English readings with additional readings in L1 about the same topic or theme.

Bilingual Dictionaries

The authors maintain that using bilingual dictionaries is one way for bilingual students to develop their vocabulary in English. They help students understand keywords that are most critical to understand the concepts they are learning. Thus, Tanzanian students can use English-Swahili dictionaries to develop their understating of key words they need to understand critical concepts.

The answer to the question as to which of these techniques may be the best for Tanzanian students will be given after discussing survey results.

Gap in the Research

As can be noted, the existing literature answers some of our research questions. However, they do so generally in a way that does not focus on the educational context of Tanzania. For instance, Celic and Seltzer (2013) discuss how translanguaging can help facilitate more effective learning of content and language by bilingual students in the state of New York. In like manner, Vladiminovna, Sergreevna, and Vladislavovna (2020) assess the cultural benefits of translanguaging using students at the American University of Sharjah as participants. Additionally, Pei-shi (2012) addresses students' attitudes towards translanguaging in Taiwan. On the other hand, Ngonyani (n.d.) analyses the factors that have contributed to the failure of the language of instruction policy in Tanzanian schools. What is special about the current study is that it seeks to explore whether translanguaging techniques that are applied in other contexts would be effective for Tanzania secondary schools. As mentioned previously, the study will be based on the beliefs and perceptions of English educators (who have been trying specific translanguaging techniques in an unauthorized manner) to ascertain the efficacy of translanguaging and determine which translanguaging techniques would be appropriate for Tanzanian students. Hence, the PI assumes this study is essential but unique to the research already accomplished in the same field.

Chapter 3

Methodology

For this qualitative study, the PI conducted an online survey among English educators in Tanzania to document and assess their beliefs and perspectives on translanguaging strategies. Hence, English educators from both private and public (government) secondary schools were the principal participants in this research.

Participants' Characteristics

To ensure the selection of participants who would best inform the research questions and enhance the understanding of the phenomenon under study, specific criteria had to be met. First, participants had to be over 18 years of age, and second, they had to have enough experience in a teaching career. As can be judged from the demographic section of the survey data, over 70% of the participants had established at least five years of experience in teaching English. This characteristic was central to the accuracy of the findings and, indeed, was in line with modern practitioners' belief that "[d]eep and significant changes in practice can only be brought about by those closest to the day-to-day work of teaching and learning" (Cochran-Smith & Lytle, 2009, p. 6).

Of the 18 participants, 3 were schooled under the English medium private school system from kindergarten through high school (early total immersion mode). At the same time, the remaining 15 went to public primary schools for the first seven years of elementary education, where Swahili was the medium before they enrolled in secondary education (late immersion mode). Consequently, the data collected reflected conflicting opinions from both categories. Additionally, every participant could communicate in English, Swahili, and at least one indigenous language. The average size of the class for each participant was 57. Further, to maintain participants' privacy and confidentiality of the data collected, English alphabets were assigned to participants in lieu of their real names. For the same reasons, Greek alphabets were assigned to the secondary schools from which participants were recruited. Table 1 summarizes the characteristics of participants.

Procedural Recruitment of Participants

First, an email was sent to the Education Director of Bukoba Diocese in Kagera, Tanzania, asking for the letter of approval to conduct research among secondary school teachers in the region. The education director oversees all the Catholic schools in the region. Upon obtaining the said letter and the Institutional Review Board (IRB) approval, the PI sent an email to principals of the aforementioned schools who, in turn, contacted select English educators and invited them to participate in the survey. The invitation included a short survey and a link to the consent document that asked them to make an informed decision about whether to participate in the research.

Second, an email was sent to the principals of select secondary schools in the Mwanza and Dar es Salaam regions asking for a letter of approval to conduct research among their teachers. Upon gaining permission to work with individual teachers and after obtaining the IRB approval, the PI emailed the select teachers inviting them to participate in the survey. The invitation included a short survey and a link to the consent document that asked them to make an informed decision about whether to participate in the research.

Region	Secondary School	Participant	Gender	Age-group	Form (Class)	Class Size	Teaching Experience (in years)
Mwanza	Alpha	A	M	41-50	1 & 2	80	10
		B	F	18-30	2 & 4	50	1
	Beta	C	M	Above 50	1 - 4	50	30
		D	F	31-40	2	47	3
	Gamma	E	M	31-40	1 & 4	50	10
		F	M	31-40	3	40	7
		G	—	41-50	1-6	80	20
Kagera	Delta	H	M	41-50	2	45	6
		I	M	18-30	4	123	5
	Epsilon	J	F	18-30	4	43	2
		K	F	31-40	1 & 3	50	10
	Zeta	L	M	18-30	4	30	2
		M	F	18-30	2	94	2
	Omega	N	M	31-40	4	40	10
		O	M	31-40	4	44	6
Dar es Salaam	Zeta	P	F	18-30	2	60	6
		Q	M	31-40	1	70	6
		R	F	41-50	3	40	7

Table 1: Participants' Characteristics

Setting and Sampling

As noted previously, this project was set in the Tanzanian context in East Africa. The Tanzanian population was estimated to be 62,716,000, based on the projections of the United Nations data. Nearly 44% of this population is under the age of 15, and this is the age group that is currently enrolled in primary and secondary education (World Population Prospectus, 2019). As of 2020, Tanzania had over 5,100 public and private secondary schools; over 2,000,000 students enrolled in secondary education program; and 106,006 registered teachers (Statistica, 2020).

The sample for this study was taken from Kagera, Mwanza, and Dar es Salaam regions. In fact, Dar es Salaam and Mwanza are the top two biggest cities with a population of 4,364,541 and 706,543, respectively. The majority of the population in these cities are Africans, with a small percentage of Europeans, Asians, and Arabs (World Population Prospectus, 2019). The African majority hail from all indigenous tribes in the country. Thus, the earmarked research sample represented the nation's tribal population and facilitated the generalization of the findings over the entire country. On the other hand, Kagera was included in the sample because it is the native region of the PI. Consequently, the PI's familiarity with the population of Kagera became a salient feature during data analysis since he could incorporate into the study his personal interpretation and understanding, cultural perspective, history, and experience.

As for the sampling design, the study followed a multistage (clustering) procedure. Accordingly, the population was divided into secondary schools based on the geographical location of the densely populated cities. Then, the PI obtained the names of individuals from those schools and finally sampled with them (Creswell & Creswell, 2018).

Region	Population	No. of Secondary Schools			No. of Teachers	Select School (Sample Population)
		Public	Private	Total		
Kagera	2,458,000	198	68	266	data not available	Epsilon
						Zeta
						Delta
						Omega
Mwanza	2,772,509	220	83	303	1,418	Beta
						Gamma
						Alpha
Dar es Salaam	4,365,000	186	138	324	3,484	Zeta

Table 2: Demographics of the Sample Population
Adapted from Multiple Online Sources

Survey Instrument

The survey instrument was created with Google Forms and comprised four elements: a) invitation to survey, b) consent letter, c) 5-Point Likert Scale, and d) open-ended questions. The first page of the survey instrument contained an invitation to teachers explaining the purpose of the survey and inviting them to participate in it. At the bottom of the email, participants were asked to indicate by checking "YES" or "NO" whether they wished to participate in the study. Those who checked "YES" were allowed to proceed to the survey; those who checked "NO" were brought to the exit page.

Additionally, the consent document informed participants that all survey questions were optional and that they were free to opt out of answering any questions if they so chose. Furthermore, the survey was exclusively anonymous, and no personally identifiable data was collected beyond the basic demographic descriptions. Even the demographic descriptions that were not pertinent to the topic under study were changed to conceal personally identifiable information. For instance, as the author noted earlier, participants were assigned English alphabet letters instead of their real names.

Data Collection

The data was collected exclusively online. The survey instrument was administered to select English educators (research participants) via email. Participants could complete the survey at their chosen location and time and could answer the questions in complete privacy. The survey was designed to take approximately 40 minutes to complete and was initially analyzed using features such as graphs, tables, and pie-charts available with Google Forms. Although the survey instrument was distributed in mid-October 2021, the response window remained open until December 21 of the same year. Hence, participants were given sufficient time to provide well-considered answers based on their experiences, perspectives, and opinions. Additionally, the survey instrument included an option to provide additional and relevant information that was not requested in the survey items. This was an alternative way of obtaining participants' additional perceptual understanding and thoughtful beliefs on the topic since, for practical reasons, interviews could not be conducted. The survey instrument follows:

Tanzania: Geographical Location of Research Samples

Investigating the Effectiveness
of Using Multiple Languages in the English Lesson

This survey instrument contains nine (9) sections: Section 1 is an Invitation to Survey; Section 2 is a Consent Document, and sections 3 through 9 contain Survey Questions. Please, read each section carefully and click NEXT at the bottom of each section for more information. At the end of the survey, remember to click or tap SUBMIT for your answers to be recorded. You have up until December 31, 2021, to complete this survey.

Invitation to Survey

My name is Thomas Kagumisa, and I am a graduate student in the department of English and Philosophy at Murray State University. You are receiving this because you teach English, and I need your help!

I am conducting a survey to investigate the effectiveness of using multiple languages in the English lesson to facilitate students' understanding. Specifically, the survey research aims to explore the English educators' beliefs and perspectives on the effectiveness of translanguaging strategies in teaching English to secondary school students in Tanzania. The survey results will help me create a project that is a culminating assignment of my program. It would be great to hear your thoughts!

If you are interested in participating in this study, please read and check "yes" on the consent document below. Then proceed to the survey by clicking NEXT. I would appreciate it if you provided well-considered answers based on your experiences, perspectives, and opinions.

Ultimately, responses to this survey may help teachers and educational policymakers develop effective methods of teaching English to secondary school students in Tanzania. You can be a part of this! Just click on NEXT and proceed to complete the survey!

Research Participation Consent Letter

Project Title: Exploring the Efficacy of Translanguaging in Teaching English to Secondary School Students in Tanzania

Principal Investigator: Thomas   Kagumisa;   tkagumisa@murraystate.edu

Faculty Sponsor: Dr. Sara Cooper; scooper19@murraystate.edu

Dear Participant,

You are being invited to participate in a research study conducted through Murray State University in Murray, Kentucky. In order to comply with federal regulations, your agreement to participate in this study is necessary. You must be at least 18 years of age to participate. Please read the form carefully and ask the Principal Investigator questions about anything that is not clear. You will be given a copy of this form to keep.

1. ***Nature and Purpose of Project***: The project aims to explore the English educators' beliefs and perspectives on the effectiveness of translanguaging strategies in teaching English to secondary school students in Tanzania. As used in this context, the terms translanguaging, multilingualism, and code meshing connote the practice of shifting from one language to another to maximize students' chances of acquiring English proficiency.

2. ***Participant Selection***: You are being asked to participate because you are an experienced English teacher, and I trust in your ability to provide helpful information on the topic under study.

3. ***Explanation of Procedures***: Upon consenting, you will be led to the page with a survey created with Google Forms. You will be asked to click on the link and answer a combination of rating scales and open-ended questions. The survey is designed to take up to 40 minutes to complete. However, the survey has no time limit; you can leave at any time and come back to it later, provided you save your responses.

4. ***Discomforts and Risks***: There are no anticipated risks and/or discomforts for participants.

5. ***Benefits***: Although the study may not benefit you directly, your participation will help me to discern the effectiveness of translanguaging strategies in the Tanzanian context, and

ultimately, propose the methods of improving instructional strategies for English educators and learners.

6. *Confidentiality*: No one will know which answers are yours. Your data will only be used in ways that do not indicate your answers or participation. Information being collected will be stored on a hard drive/server secured by passwords. The information will be kept for at least three years following the conclusion of the study period. After that, the files will be deleted.

7. *Refusal/Withdrawal*: Your participation is strictly voluntary, and you are free to withdraw, stop participating at any time, or opt-out of answering any question with absolutely no penalty.

8. *Contact Information*: Any questions about the procedures or conduct of this research should be brought to the attention of Thomas Kagumisa at tkagumisa@murraystate.edu. If you would like to know the results of this study, please contact Thomas Kagumisa using the above contact information.

Your signature indicates that this study has been explained to you, that your questions have been answered, and that you agree to take part in this study.

The dated approval stamp on this document indicates that this project has been reviewed and approved by the Murray State University Institutional Review Board (IRB) for the Protection of Human Subjects. If you have any questions about your rights as a research participant, you should contact the MSU IRB Coordinator at +1(270) 809-2916 or msu.irb@murraystate.edu.

Thank you kindly for your cooperation.

Sincerely,

Thomas Kagumisa

Dated Stamp

MURRAY STATE
UNIVERSITY
Institutional Review Board
Approved: 10/15/21 Expires: 10/14/22

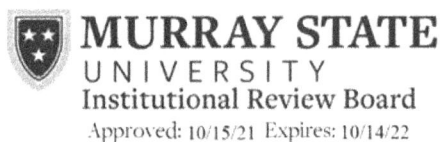

By checking "YES" you will be formally signing the consent document and allowed to proceed to survey questions. If you check "NO" you will be led to the "SUBMIT" option.

- o   Yes, I wish to participate in the study.
- o   No, I do not wish to participate in the study.

Survey Questions for Teachers at All Select Secondary Schools in Tanzania

Note: The terms *translanguaging* and *code meshing* are used interchangeably in this survey to connote the practice of alternating between English and Swahili to maximize the chances of students' acquisition of English skills.

A. Demographic Information

1. Your Name (Optional): _____
2. Gender (Optional): _____
3. School Name and Address: _____
4. Class (Form) You Teach: _____
5. Average No. of Students in Class: _____
6. Years of Teaching Experience: _____

B. Teachers' Translanguaging Practices

1. *Directions*: Indicate the extent to which the following statements apply to your strategies of teaching English and/or other subjects. Click or tap the most correct answer on a 5-point Likert-type scale.

   a) I alternate between English and Swahili when I am teaching. [Never, Seldom, Occasionally, Frequently, Always]

   b) I allow my students to use either English or Swahili when responding to questions in class. [Never, Seldom, Occasionally, Frequently, Always]

   c) Our principal encourages the use of both English and Swahili during classroom instruction. [Never, Seldom, Occasionally, Frequently, Always]

2. *Directions*: Provide a short narrative answer to the following questions.

    a) What are the two most important practices you use to help your students understand the English lesson?

    b) Could students' achievement improve if translanguaging strategies were completely excluded from practice? Explain.

C. Teachers' Core-Beliefs on the Effectiveness of Translanguaging

1. *Directions*: Describe the extent to which you agree or disagree with the following statements: Click or tap the most correct answer on a 5-point Likert-type scale.

    a) My students comprehend the lesson better when I alternate between English and Swahili than when I use English only. [Strongly Disagree, Disagree, Neutral, Agree, Strongly Agree]

    b) I am aware that translanguaging strategies create a carefree classroom atmosphere and decrease anxiety. [Strongly Disagree, Disagree, Neutral, Agree, Strongly Agree]

    c) Rather than insisting on the monolingual (English only) policy, the Ministry of Education should allow teachers to use both Swahili and English as languages of instruction. [Strongly Disagree, Disagree, Neutral, Agree, Strongly Agree]

2. *Directions*: Provide a short narrative answer to the following questions.

   a) What do you think would be the outcome in terms of students' performance if both Swahili and English were officially authorized as languages of instruction in all subject areas?

   b) Based on your own teaching experience, describe the extent to which translanguaging instructional strategies are effective.

D. Teachers' Perception of Students' Attitudes Toward Translanguaging

1. *Directions*: Indicate the extent to which the following statements apply to your students' attitudes with respect to translanguaging strategies. Click or tap the most correct answer on a 5-point Likert-type scale.

   a) My students admit that they understand my lesson better when I explain certain concepts in Swahili. [Never, Seldom, Sometimes, Often, Always]

   b) My students become active in class when I alternate between English and Swahili. [Never, Seldom, Sometimes, Often, Always]

   c) My students display satisfaction and less stress when I use Swahili to clarify the meaning of words and phrases. [Never, Seldom, Sometimes, Often, Always]

2. *Directions*: Provide a short narrative answer to the following questions.
   a) Would you recommend translanguaging strategies to other English teachers? Why?
   b) How would you use translanguaging strategies to improve students' attitudes to the English lesson?

E. Teachers' Perspectives on the English Only Policy

1. *Directions*: Describe the extent to which you agree or disagree with the following statements: Click or tap the most correct answer on a 5-point Likert-type scale.
   a) Switching from one language to another suggests the teacher's lack of proficiency in English.
      [Strongly Disagree, Disagree, Neutral, Agree, Strongly Agree]
   b) Code meshing (alternating from one language to another) confuses students, impedes their acquisition of English, and therefore, should be avoided.
      [Strongly Disagree, Disagree, Neutral, Agree, Strongly Agree]
   c) Using English only during instruction provides more exposure to English and more chances to acquiring it. [Strongly Disagree, Disagree, Neutral, Agree, Strongly Agree]
2. *Directions*: Provide a short narrative answer to the following questions.

a) Did you do your studies at the school where the policy was "English-only"? What was your experience?

b) Briefly discuss other English-only beliefs that you might have.

F. **Teachers' Perspectives on the Cultural Beliefs with Respect to Translanguaging**

1. *Directions*: Describe the extent to which you agree or disagree with the following statements: Click or tap the most correct answer on a 5-point Likert-type scale.

   a) I am aware that when I speak English fluently (without code meshing), I command the respect of my students and acquaintances. [Strongly Disagree, Disagree, Neutral, Agree, Strongly Agree]

   b) I am aware of the public opinion that fluency in English is associated with a high level of education. [Strongly Disagree, Disagree, Neutral, Agree, Strongly Agree]

   c) Insisting on an English Only Policy is an attempt to adapt students to the western world and alienate them from their own people and culture. [Strongly Disagree, Disagree, Neutral, Agree, Strongly Agree]

2. *Directions*: Provide a short narrative answer to the following questions.

   a) Comment on the following statement: "Since culture is produced primarily via language, endows experience with meaning, and provides a deeply held

sense of identity and social belonging, translanguaging between English and Swahili should be allowed for the sake of Tanzanians' sense of self-
worth."

b) Briefly discuss any other cultural beliefs on translanguaging that are not addressed by the items
above.

G. Translanguaging Techniques

1. *Directions*: Indicate the extent to which the following
   statements apply to your translanguaging strategies.
   Click or tap the most correct answer on a 5-point Likert-type scale.
   a) My students use both English and Swahili during
      group discussions. [Never, Seldom, Occasionally,
      Frequently, Always]
   b) I use an insertional strategy (intra-sentential) dur-
      ing classroom instruction by incorporating a few
      Swahili words in a predominantly English speech.
      [Never, Seldom, Occasionally, Frequently, Always]
   c) I use an alternational method (inter-sentential) dur-
      ing classroom instruction by delivering part of my
      speech in English, and part in Swahili. [Never, Sel-
      dom, Occasionally, Frequently, Always]
2. *Directions*: Provide a short narrative answer to the following questions.

a) Describe the extent to which these strategies have proven effective.

b) What other strategies would you recommend?

Data Coding and Analysis

The greater part of the survey instrument comprised of Likert-Scale items that were used to measure participants' attitudes to a particular question or statement. As can be imagined, Likert scale data is not always easy to analyze and interpret since one cannot use the mean to measure central tendency. For instance, we cannot calculate the average of "Frequently," "Always," and "Occasionally." To overcome this difficulty, the data was converted into bar-graphs. The numerical heights of the bar-graph clearly demonstrated the scope of participants' attitude to a particular statement. For example, in Graph 2, 8 participants said *never* and 5 said *seldom* to the statement "I alternate between English and Swahili when I am teaching."

Every so often, however, the PI had to think carefully about the nature of the question and draw reasonable inferences from responses given by participants. This approach was particularly applicable when a specific item elicited somewhat homogeneous responses from participants. For example, when participants were asked to indicate their level of agreement to the statement, "Translanguaging confuses students, impedes their acquisition of English, and therefore should be avoided," 40% of participants strongly disagreed, while 26.70% disagreed (cfr. Pie-Chart 2). In that case, the inferential statement was "Most participants did not

assent to the belief that translanguaging confuses students …"
However, responses that were ascribed an extremely high percentage were analyzed independently.

Besides bar-graphs, pie-charts were also used to facilitate data
analysis and interpretation. These figures were essential in showing
the part-to-whole relationship of a particular data category. Additionally, tables were used to organize data that appeared too detailed to be described adequately in text. This was true for participants' characteristics, as shown in Table 1 above. On the other
hand, it was easy to analyze and make sense of the essay-type responses. Essay-type responses that provided closely related opinions were categorized and paraphrased accordingly.

Research Approval

Since the research protocol involved human subjects, the PI
completed the CITI training to educate himself on the protection
of research participants. After obtaining the certificate for CITI
program course, the PI completed and submitted the application
form for the Institutional Review Board (IRB) approval. After affirming that the research would not violate subjects' rights and that
it conforms to the Code of Federal Regulations, the IRB granted the
approval.

Furthermore, the research was authorized by the principals of
secondary schools from which the participants were recruited.
However, the research did not require local review since Tanzania
has no such requirement. Hence, the PI obtained a Memo of Cultural Appropriateness from a local authority and a letter

confirming that an ethical review is not required. Finally, the informed consent was obtained from every participant as per the approved IRB application protocols.

Validity Strategies

Multiple validity procedures were followed to minimize the potential bias and increase the standard of accuracy and reliability of the findings. First, a detailed description of the findings was provided to bring the readers to the research context and to give them an element of shared experiences and multiple perspectives about the topic. Second, the bias that the PI brought to the study was clarified. For instance, under the subtitle "Sampling and Setting," the PI mentioned that the Kagera region was included in the research sample because it is his native area. As a result, the PI's familiarity with the population of Kagera became a salient feature during data analysis since he could incorporate into the study his personal interpretation and understanding, cultural perspective, history, and experience. This explanation helps to let the reader know that the interpretation of the findings is partly shaped by the PI's background and creates an open and honest narrative that resonates well with the readers. Third, negative and discrepant information that contradicted the topic under study was presented and discussed accordingly to make an account more realistic and valid. Fourth, the project was discussed by research group members at every stage to make it resonate with people other than the PI. Finally, the project was reviewed by a peer who was not a research group member and not familiar with the topic. This independent reviewer looked over many aspects of the project and enhanced the study's overall validity (Creswell & Creswell, 2018).

Conclusion

Since the study's intent was to generate perspectives, opinions, and beliefs from participants on the phenomenon of translanguaging, the qualitative methodologies discussed in this chapter appeared to be the fitting option. As might have been noted, the PI relied exclusively on the survey for data collection. Qualitative interviews could have enhanced an in-depth exploration of participants' thoughts, feelings, and understandings on the topic, but challenges of distance and poor internet connectivity precipitated the possibility of this option. However, every set of Likert-type items in the survey instrument was paired with at least two open-ended questions to fill the vacuum that the absence of interviews might have created. For the most part, however, the combination of the methodology protocols that have been observed serves to attest to the credibility of the study's findings, conclusions, and recommendations.

Chapter 4

Research Findings

This chapter presents survey results of the phenomenological study conducted to answer the research question: *What are Tanzanian educators' core beliefs and perspectives related to the effectiveness of translanguaging strategies in teaching English as a Foreign Language (EFL) to secondary school students?* However, to narrow the focus of the study and facilitate the process of data collection, the central research question was broken down into seven more sub-questions, namely:

1. Do you apply translanguaging methods in your English class? If your answer is affirmative, explain the manner and the extent to which you practice the strategies.
2. What are your core-beliefs, suggestions, and perspectives with regard to the effectiveness of translanguaging practices?
3. How do students respond to the incorporation of other languages in the EFL lesson?
4. What are your beliefs and perspectives on the English Only Policy?
5. What socio-cultural beliefs do people associate with translanguaging strategies?

6. Might students use the translanguaging approach at the same time manage to think in the target language (English) with minimal interference from their native language(s)?

7. What translanguaging methods can we use to effect teaching and learning English as a Foreign Language (EFL)?

Correspondingly, the entire chapter and the survey results were organized into seven themes in tune with the number of research sub-questions.

For the most part, the data collected was the result of the participants' responses on the 5-point Likert-type scale, on which they appropriately indicated the extent to which the statement applies to their practice of teaching English or their beliefs as far as using translanguaging strategies goes. Under each set of Likert scale results is a pie-chart, graphic, or tabular representation of the same results. The purpose was not to duplicate the results but to provide the reader with visual elements; thus, facilitating an understanding of emerging trends and relationships in the survey findings.

Aside from the Likert scale, participants were asked to attend to restricted-response essay-type questions. The purpose was to elicit elaborative information that could not be obtained through the Likert-Scale. To demonstrate the validity and impartiality of data coding, the direct quotations from participants were rewritten in a verbatim style. This approach also served to reflect the language variety that does not always adhere to standard written English.

In essence, the chapter presents a brief report and synthesis of survey results concerning the phenomenon under study. For that reason, any evaluative, speculative, interpretative, or critical information is reserved for the discussion and recommendations chapter that will follow next.

Research Sub-Question 1: Do you apply translanguaging methods in your English class? If your answer is affirmative, explain the manner and the extent to which you practice the strategies.

The first question in the survey instrument focused on how and the extent to which teachers apply translanguaging practices as they teach English or other subjects. Survey results are categorized into two sub-themes: Results from the 5-Point Likert-Scale and responses to extended answer essay questions.

Responses from the 5-Point Likert Scale

When asked to tell how often they alternate between English and Swahili during classroom instruction, 7 out of 15 participants said they do so *occasionally*, while 4 said *seldom*, 2 *always*, 1 *frequently*, and 1 *never*. However, 3 participants declined to answer the question. As can be observed, the highest number of participants admitted that they use the method occasionally. Nevertheless, most of the participants (8) claimed that they *never* allow their students to alternate between languages when responding to questions in class. Only 2 participants agreed that they *always* allow, and 5 *seldom* allow their students to do so. The rest of the participants abstained from answering the question. On the other hand, when asked whether principals allow the use of both English and Swahili during classroom instruction, 7 participants said *never*, 4 said *seldom*, 3 said *occasionally*, and 1 said *frequently*. Graph 1 represents the summary of participants' responses regarding teachers' translanguaging practices.

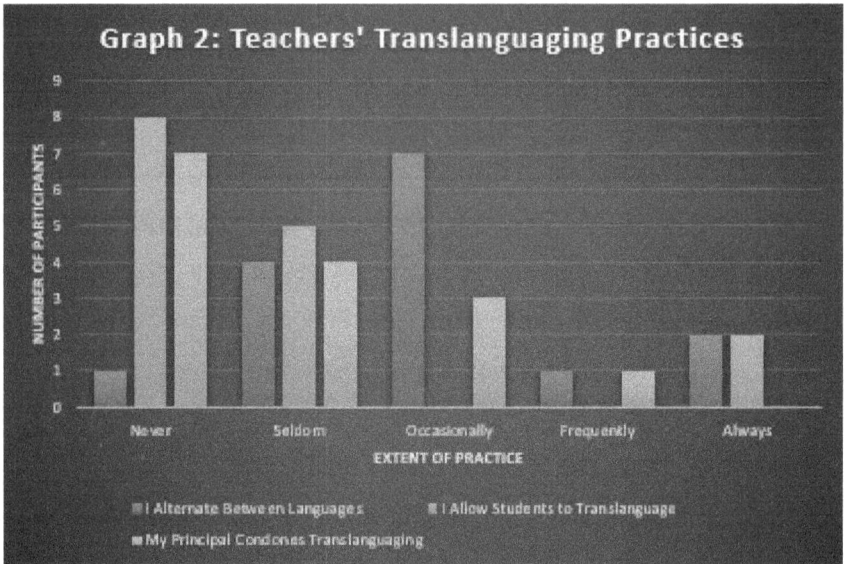

Graph 2: Teachers' Translanguaging Practices

Responses to the Restricted-Answer Essay Questions

As a way of helping students understand the English lesson, the majority of participants specified that they encourage students to speak English all the time, participate in English clubs, essay writing activities, and debating activities, and use teaching aids, to name a few examples. Precisely, participant K stated:

First, I make good friendship with my students during the lesson and out of class hours. That friendship help my students to have self-confidence to talk with me and ask anything she/he doesn't understand. Second, I insist my student to find new vocabularies and their meaning not less than five words and write down in their notebook everyday and i do inspection for each students on Friday. That practice help them to understand many words of English language and help students to have bank of words in their brains. [sic]

On the other hand, participants' general opinion on whether students' achievement could improve if translanguaging practices were completely banned from use was negative. Some went a step further to clarify: "In fact, the performance would go down because some students have a low command of the English language. I have experienced cases where a students asks for the explanation to be repeated in Swahili having not understood when English was purely used." In the same vein, another participant stated: "No, because most of students have not good foundation in English language. Therefore if the teacher exclude[s] strategies of translanguaging [a] large group of students will not understand just like to play music in the jungle and expect animals to enjoy it." Despite the disparity of opinions on this sub-question, the highest number of participants affirmed using translanguaging practices and indicated the manner and the extent to which they apply the method.

Research Sub-Question 2: What are your core-beliefs, suggestions, and perspectives with regard to the effectiveness of translanguaging practices?

In this sub-question, participants were asked to explain what they believe about translanguaging strategies as well as their perspectives and suggestions on the strategies.

Responses from the 5-Point Likert Scale

Specifically, participants were asked to explain if students comprehend the lesson better when the teacher alternates between English and Swahili than when English only is used. Out of 15 participants, 8 responded affirmatively (agreed), 1 strongly agreed, 2 disagreed, 2 strongly disagreed while 2 remained neutral. Therefore, on this element, the highest number of participants confirmed that translanguaging facilitates lesson comprehension in the Tanzanian context. Similarly, most of participants admitted that they are aware that translanguaging strategies create a carefree classroom atmosphere and decrease anxiety. This was shown by survey results whereby 8 participants agreed, 1 strongly agreed, 3 disagreed, and 2 strongly disagreed to the statement. Contrastingly, there was a unanimous disagreement about whether translanguaging should replace the monolingual policy. For instance, when asked to give their opinion on the statement, "Rather than insisting on the monolingual (English Only) policy, the Ministry of Education should allow teachers to use both Swahili and English as official languages of instruction," 7 out of 15 participants strongly disagreed, 1 disagreed, 1 remained neutral, 6 agreed, and 1 strongly agreed. Thus, although the highest number of participants affirmed that translanguaging facilitates lesson comprehension and creates a conducive classroom atmosphere, the same participants were not content with having translanguaging as an official policy of education.

Responses to Restricted-Answer Essay Questions

Participants' core beliefs on the effectiveness of translanguaging became more apparent in their responses to open-ended questions on the survey instrument. Under this section, question one asked participants to explain what they think would be the outcome of students' performance if both Swahili and English were officially authorized as languages of instruction. Some participants commented positively, saying that students' performance would improve and that students would understand the lesson clearly and none would be left behind on the ground of language barrier. Specifically, participant K stated, "I believe that this will create [a] greater chance of understanding the subjects and increase the chances of passing the examinations and therefore will help to produce competent candidates." However, some participants detailed negative beliefs in response to the question. Some said that the outcome would be poor performance and attributed the poor performance of Tanzanian students to informal use of translanguaging strategies. Others believed that Swahili would dominate classroom instruction, eventually undermining students' competence in English. Still, others thought students' writing would be nothing but a haphazard mix of English and Swahili grammar. As an illustration, participant N stated: "May cause students to use codemixing when they want to answer school exams or national exams." In brief, this question elicited conflicting views from participants.

Question two of this section stated: "Based on your teaching experience, describe the extent to which translanguaging strategies are effective." Contrary to what was said regarding the previous

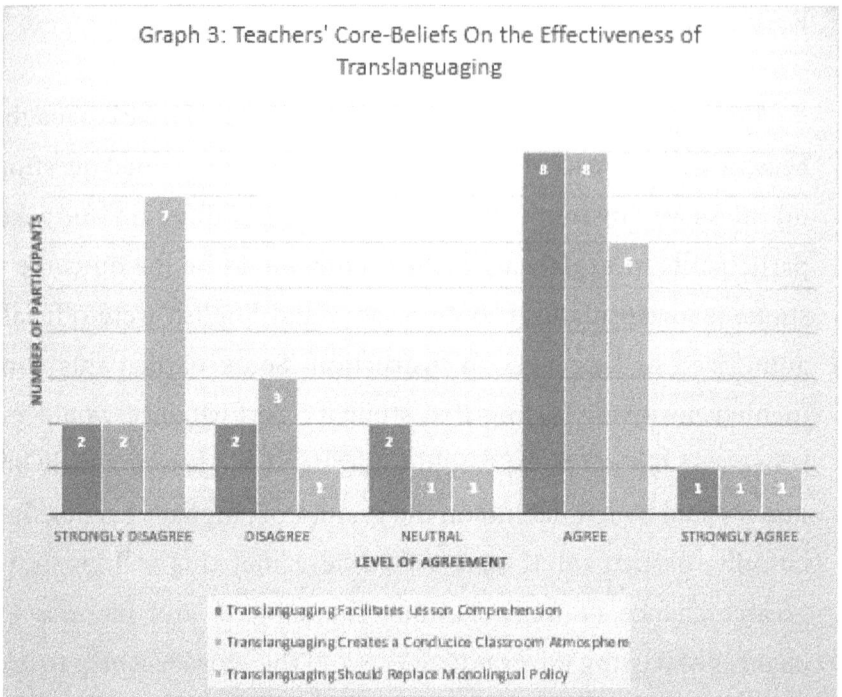

Graph 3: Teachers' Core-Beliefs On the Effectiveness of Translanguaging

question, the overwhelming number of participants responded affirmatively, crediting the effectiveness of translanguaging strategies thereby. For instance, out of 16 participants, 15 commented variously that translanguaging strategies encourage learning activities, reinforce understanding and association, help clarify vocabularies and complex terms, facilitate active classroom participation, and support students who lack a solid foundation in English. Notably, participant P clarified, "Translanguaging instructional strategies are very effective as they bring in the sense of inclusiveness. It should be borne in mind that some students have [a] poor English basis and thus low mastery of language. Therefore, occasionally switching to languages they master, makes them feel involved and

increases their understanding of the lessons." Identically, participant G pointed out: "Effectiveness of translanguaging depends on
the class level whereby its [sic] more effective in lower levels of education especially form one and two but from form three single language does not hinder learning process to a greater extent." Only
one participant departed from the majority opinion and said, "They
[translanguaging strategies] are not effective in the case of the performance of the student."

**Research Sub-Question 3: How do students respond to the incor-
poration of other languages in the EFL lesson?**

The central focus of this question was to examine teachers' perceptions of students' attitudes toward the incorporation of Swahili
in an English lesson. Like in the previous sub-sections, responses to
this question will be reported under two headings: Likert scale and
restricted response essay questions.

Responses from the 5-Point Likert Scale

The first item on the Likert scale was whether students understand the lesson better when the teacher explains certain concepts
in Swahili. Results showed that most students understand the lesson better when translanguaging strategies are used. This was
proved by the highest percentage of participants (44%) who selected *sometimes* and the second-highest (19%) who selected *often*.
However, 12% of participants said students *never*, 13% said *seldom*,
while 12% said *always* understand the lesson better when Swahili is
used to explain certain concepts. To the second statement, "My

Students become active when I alternate between English and Swahili," 44% of participants said *sometimes*, 25% said *often* while 19% said *always*. These were the highest percentages that were ascribed affirmatively to the statement. Only 6% of participants said *never* and 6% said *seldom* to the same statement.

The last question under this section intended to determine whether students display satisfaction and less stress when the teacher uses Swahili to clarify the meaning of words and phrases. The results showed that the highest percentage (38%) of participants' students *always* display satisfaction and less stress, while 25% *often*, 13% *sometimes* 6% *seldom*, and 19% *never* display the same attitudes. Although participants provided varying and somewhat contradictory responses, the dominant opinion is that students exhibit positive attitudes toward translanguaging strategies. The summary of the findings for this section is provided in Table 3 below.

Student Attitude toward Translanguaging	Extent to Which the Attitude is Manifested				
	Never	Seldom	Sometimes	Often	Always
Students Admit Their Better Understanding of the Lesson When I Translanguage	12%	13%	44%	19%	12%
Students Become Active in Class When I Translanguage	6%	6%	44%	25%	19%
Students Display Satisfaction & Less Stress When I Translanguage	19%	6%	12%	25%	38%

Table 3: Teachers' Perception of Students' Attitudes towards Translanguaging Strategies

Responses to Restricted-Answer Essay Questions

The first question under this section required participants to explain whether they would recommend translanguaging strategies to other English teachers. Several participants said they would recommend using translanguaging strategies to other teachers because most secondary school students hail from public primary schools where Swahili is the medium of instruction. Thus, as they transition to secondary education, English becomes a barrier to lesson comprehension due to a lack of a solid foundation in the language. Participants said translanguaging could help students break through linguistic hurdles in that context. Other participants recommended translanguaging strategies to English teachers who teach the lower classes in order to help create an anxiety-free learning environment. They argued that the EOP should be maintained in higher classes to give students adequate exposure to the language. Also, participants maintained that other teachers should adopt translanguaging strategies since they augment the level of understanding and give students the freedom to express themselves. However, participants advised that the use of Swahili should not dominate the instruction lest it undermine students' ability to achieve fluency in English.

Nevertheless, some participants were opposed to the idea of recommending the use of translanguaging strategies to other teachers. For instance, participant D said, "No. Teachers should find best ways of teaching English language without basing on translanguaging." Similarly, participant G replied, "No. because [sic] it creates a direct translated grammar which is harmful to English teaching and learning." Also, participant G discredited translanguaging on the ground that "[i]t doesn't help students master the language." Nevertheless, despite the negative responses, most participants supported the idea of recommending translanguaging strategies to other English educators.

Responses to question two (How would you use translanguaging strategies to improve students' attitudes to the English lesson?) reflected yet another set of conflicting views. Some said they would give students a chance to use Swahili in asking for clarification of difficult terms as a way of helping them participate actively in class; whereas, others said they would encourage students to use English-Swahili dictionaries; explain concepts in English then switch to Swahili; use translanguaging strategies only when there is a need to clarify difficult concepts—to name a few examples. Uniquely, one participant clarified by saying, "I will always remind students that English is a global language [and] that they cannot avoid as it connects the world and telling them that when I have to use Swahili it is because I wouldn't find any better means to clarify what I had to clarify in Swahili."

Adversely, some participants dismissed altogether the idea of using translanguaging strategies to improve students' attitudes toward the English lesson. As an illustration, participant A said, "Actually, I would not invite this again in teaching, because by my experience, students enjoys a good flow of language." Similarly, participant B stated, "It should be last alternative after other efforts have proved failure," whereas participant D said she does not prefer translanguaging strategies at all.

Like what was observed in the previous sections, the positive things said by participants about using translanguaging strategies to boost students' attitudes to the English lesson outweigh the negative ones.

Research Sub-Question 4: What are English educators' beliefs and perspectives on the English Only Policy?

Question four was intended to determine teachers' perspectives on the English Only Policy. Responses to both the restricted-answer essay questions and the Likert Scale reveal participants' different opinions on the question.

Responses from the 5-Point Likert Scale

Pursuant to the majority opinion, participants denied the contention that switching from one language to another suggests the teacher's lack of proficiency in English (33.3% disagreed while 33.3% strongly disagreed—refer to pie-chart 1). Similarly, participants disagreed with the belief that code-switching (alternating from one language to another) confuses students and impedes their acquisition of English. Pie-chart 2 shows that 26.70% of participants disagreed while 40% strongly disagreed. Finally, participants concurred that using English only during instruction provides more exposure to English and more chances to acquiring it. This was proven by the results on pie-chart 3 whereby 26.60% of participants agreed, and 46.70% strongly agreed with the statement.

PIE-CHART 1: SWITCHING FROM ONE LANGUAGE TO ANOTHER
SUGGESTS THE TEACHER'S LACK OF PROFICIENCY IN ENGLISH

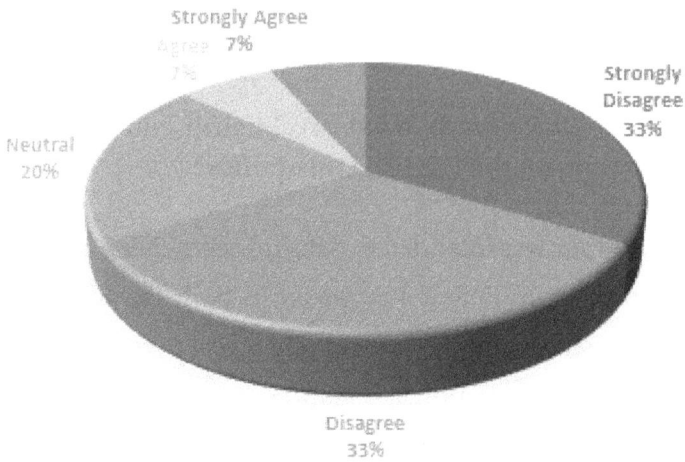

Strongly Agree
Agree 7%
7%

Neutral
20%

Strongly
Disagree
33%

Disagree
33%

Pie-Chart 2: Translanguaging Confuses Students, Impedes their
Acquisition of English, and Therefore, Should be Avoided.

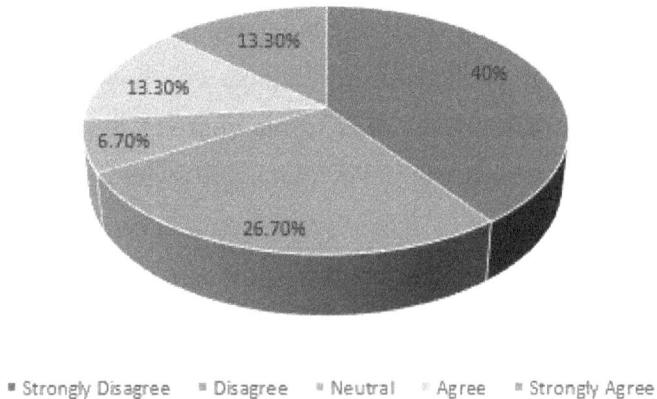

13.30%

13.30%

6.70%

40%

26.70%

■ Strongly Disagree   ■ Disagree   ■ Neutral   Agree   ■ Strongly Agree

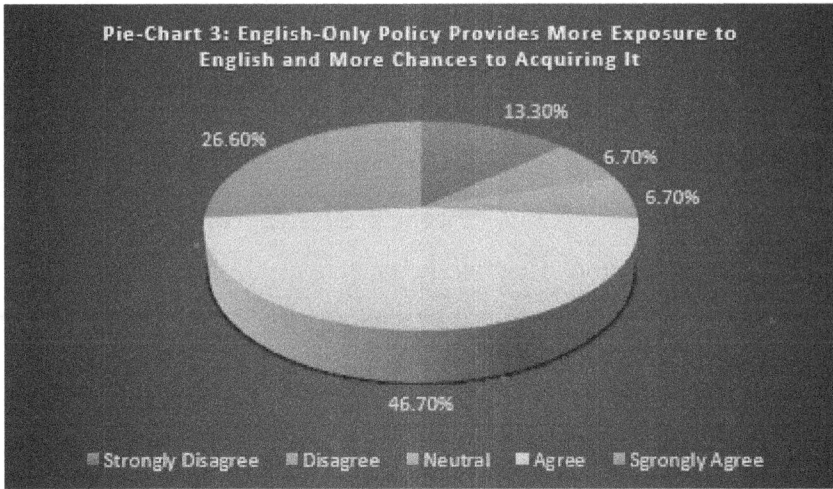

Pie-Chart 3: English-Only Policy Provides More Exposure to English and More Chances to Acquiring It

13.30%
26.60%
6.70%
6.70%
46.70%

■ Strongly Disagree   ■ Disagree   ■ Neutral   ■ Agree   ■ Sgrongly Agree

Responses to Restricted-Answer Essay Questions

Essay question 1 stated: "Did you take your studies at the school where the language of instruction was English only? What was your experience?" In response, participant A said "Yes" but added that she had to work hard on her own to acquire English skills. Also, participant B admitted having been educated under the EOP and attributed his failure in English to that policy. Uniformly, participant C said "Yes" and commented that teachers were often violating the policy by using translanguaging strategies. Similar views were shared by participant D, who said: "Yes, Though long time ago my English teacher used also Swahili and sometimes vernacular words making the class to understand. for instance, when teaching about tenses and types of conditional sentences." [sic] On the other hand, participant E admitted having been schooled under the same policy but recalled, "The response was very low due to lack of vo-cabularies." Identically, participant F agreed to have schooled under EOP but observed that there were instances of code-meshing and that this helped students understand the content.

Conversely, some participants admitted having been educated under the EOP but commented positively on the policy. For instance, participant G said that the policy helped him to learn English in a short time. Meanwhile, participant H said, "Yes, I did. It was easy for me to learn and understand because I had good basis of English language that I had acquired in my lower levels of schooling." Correspondingly, other participants appreciated the EOP, saying that it was very effective and helped give them a solid foundation and fluency in English.

When asked to "[b]riefly discuss other English-only beliefs that you might have," some participants said that using an English Only Policy would undermine the strength of our national language (Swahili). Others remarked that EOP causes tension and a stressful atmosphere; it creates fear and lack of confidence, especially among students who hail from government school; others advised that it should be applied from kindergarten through college level to give students a solid foundation in the language. Precisely, one participant stated:

> Denying learners the translanguaging platform in their course of learning makes some of them fail to perform in their studies as they can't express what they know or can do. Some have failed in exams not because they know little or nothing of what they were taught but because they can't express what they know in English.

Contrastingly, some minority participants argued positively on the topic. They maintained that applying EOP will enable students to master the language; will help students integrate with people from other countries; will "[m]ake students learn from their teachers and create a desire for students to be like their teachers."

All things considered, participants had opposing ideas on the two questions discussed in this section. Nevertheless, the majority did not comment in favor of the EOP.

Research Sub-Question 5: What socio-cultural beliefs do people associate with translanguaging strategies?

Question 5 was intended to investigate teachers' perspectives on socio-cultural beliefs with respect to translanguaging strategies. In keeping with the previous approach, the findings of this section are summarized under two sub-headings: responses from the Likert scale and responses to restricted-answer essay questions.

Responses to the 5-Point Likert Scale

One of the socio-cultural beliefs regarding translanguaging strategies is that "[t]he teacher who is fluent in English commands respect from students and acquaintances." The highest percentages of participants (26.6% *strongly agree* and 40% *agree*) affirmed the truth of the statement. Meanwhile, 6.6% disagreed, whereas another 6.6% dismissed the belief as irrelevant. The second belief was that fluency in English is associated with a high level of education. Twenty-five percent of participants agreed, while 18.7% strongly agreed. On the other hand, 31.3% disagreed, 12.5% strongly dis-

agreed, and 12.5% chose to remain neutral. Next was the belief that
"[i]nsisting on the EOP is an attempt to adapt students to the western world and alienate them from their own people and culture."
Again, the highest percentage of participants did not consider this
belief valid: 33.3% disagreed, while 20% strongly disagreed. However, 26.6% agreed to the statement, 13.3% strongly agreed, while
6.6% remained neutral. Generally speaking, the survey results confirmed the popular socio-cultural beliefs about translanguaging.
The summary of these results is presented in graph 3 below.

Graph 4: Teachers' Perspectives on Socio-Cultural Beliefs With Respect to Translanguaging

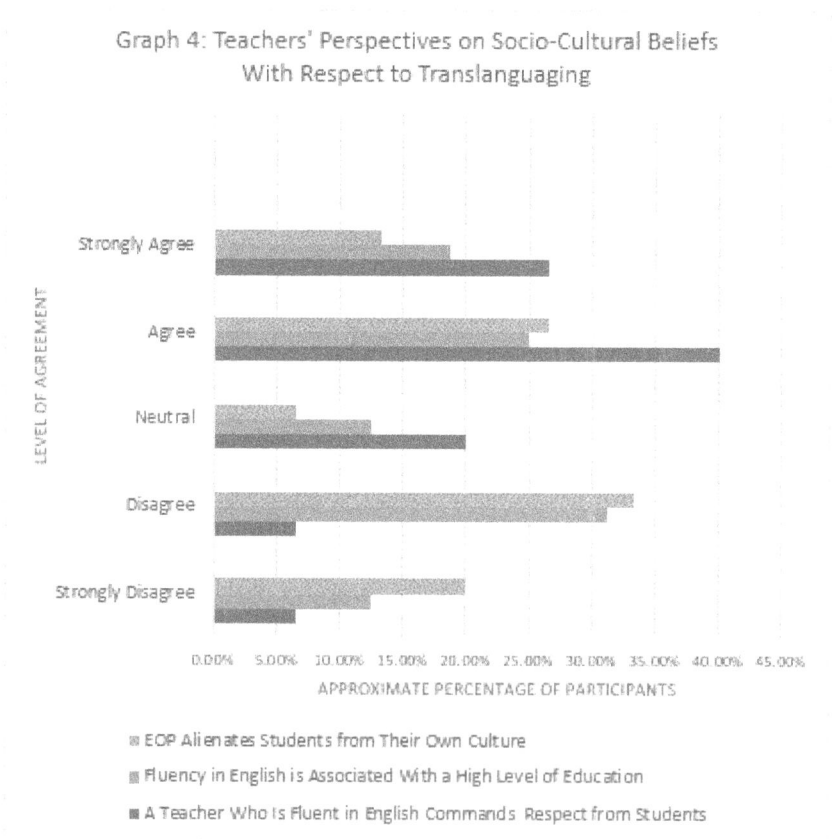

Responses to Restricted-Answer Essay Questions

In question 1, participants were asked to comment on the following statement: "Since culture is produced primarily via language, endows experience with meaning, and provides a deeply
held sense of identity and social belonging, translanguaging between English and Swahili should be allowed for the sake of Tanzanians' sense of self-worth." Fifty percent of participants commented in agreement with the statement. They supported the use
of both Swahili and English to secure the nation's culture and enable Tanzanians to participate in international trade, tourism, diplomacy, etc. Specifically, participant C maintained that "Translanguaging between English and Swahili will pull up our culture because ... in today's world most of Tanzanians value English and
Swahili language. And a person who knows how to speak English
is regarded as an educated one." Likewise, participant G pointed
out that "[i]n order to promote our culture, translanguaging should
be allowed because in Tanzania both languages [Swahili and Eng-
lish] are official."

Unlike the participants quoted above, participants F, G, M, and
L proposed the monolingual method (EOP) in lieu of translanguaging. In particular, participant F said that we should endorse English
only because it gives students self-confidence as well as a sense of
self-worth. G insisted that Swahili should be used at all levels of education and communication since it is our national language. M
argued, "For the sake of creating self-worth and identity in Tanzania, Kiswahili should be used in education and other activities."
Other participants gave ambiguous responses that indicated they

did not understand the question correctly. For instance, N said, "Yes, but Swahili is there are our bilingual, English should be taught for people to match the new world of science and technology." Similarly, P claimed that "[translanguaging] should be because some [of] the students have been affected by our mother tongue." In essence, the majority opinion is that the use of both English and Swahili during classroom instruction helps to promote the sense of self-worth among Tanzania students.

In question 2, participants were asked to briefly discuss any other socio-cultural beliefs that were not addressed by the items on the Likert scale. Their remarks reflected a diversity of opinions on the topic. On the positive side, participants Q, R, and S thought that Swahili should be used side by side with English to preserve the national identity and traditional customs. Negatively, participant K argued, "It is believed that the EOP is a form of neo-colonialism that is pushed by [the] western world aimed at wiping out our local languages and slowly making our nation dependent upon western civilization." They also felt that translanguaging is associated with prestige and intellectual pride.

Research Sub-Question 6: Might students use the translanguaging approach at the same time manage to think in the target language (English) with minimal interference from their native language(s)?

This question was answered in the literature review chapter and, therefore, was excluded from the survey instrument. In fact, the existing research proved that since students do not start by thinking in English, allowing for the exploration of ideas in Swahili supports a gradual, developmental process in which the use of Swahili languages drops off naturally as they become less necessary (Auerbach, 1993). Thus, enforcing the English Only Policy is tantamount to neglecting the fact that a Tanzanian student's thinking, feeling, and artistic life are very much rooted in Swahili and their mother tongues.

Research Sub-Question 7: What translanguaging methods can we use to effect teaching and learning English as a Foreign Language (EFL)?

The purpose of the final sub-question was to collect information from participants regarding the effective methods and techniques of translanguaging. In that case, participants were requested to indicate on the Likert scale the extent to which the three select techniques apply to their translanguaging strategies.

Responses to the 5-Point Likert Scale

The first item on the Likert scale asked the participant to indicate whether they allow students to use both English and Swahili during group discussions. The highest number of participants (40%) said they *sometimes* use the method, while 20% said they do so only *occasionally*. Additionally, 20% said they *always* use the method. On the other hand, 13.3% said they *often* do so, whereas 6.6% said they *never* use the method.

Item two was intended to examine whether English teachers use an insertional (Intrasentential) strategy by incorporating a few Swahili words in a predominantly English speech. On a Likert scale, those who *sometimes* use this technique comprise the highest percentage (62.5%). Other options were ascribed to a meager percentage.

The final item asked whether the teachers use alternational (Intersentential) techniques, that is, delivering part of the speech in English and part of it in Swahili. The responses to this item seem to overlap. Forty three percent said they *never* whereas another 43.7% said *sometimes* they use the technique. Again, other options were accorded low percentages. The results of these items are summarized in graph 4 below.

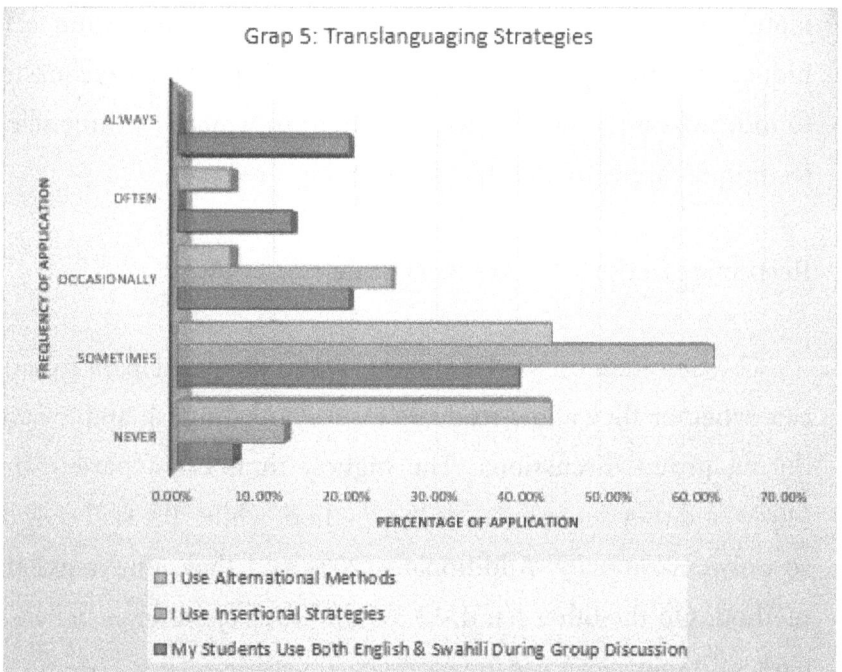

Grap 5: Translanguaging Strategies

Responses to Restricted-Answer Essay Questions

First, participants were asked to describe how effective the strategies/methods itemized in the above section are. In response, participants commented both positively and negatively. Out of 16 participants, 12 commented positively, saying that the strategies help students understand new vocabularies and terms, augment classroom instruction, clarify the lesson content, help students comprehend the lesson, and facilitate verbal communication between students and teachers. One of the participants clarified: "The strategies have proven very effective because they make all students understand the lesson irrespective of the differences in their mastery of the English language." Similarly, another participant remarked, "These strategies have proven effective from primary school, secondary school, as well as high school levels of education because many students have problems in English language."

Only two students made negative remarks on this question. One believed that "[m]ultilingual in teaching and learning have proven weak, since teachers fall in a heavy duty of insisting the use of English in communication at school." Another one said, "The strategy of using Swahili and English have proven [a] failure because of the fact that it led to the poor performance to the student." Despite these last two remarks, survey results show that translanguaging strategies are effective.

To know more about translanguaging strategies that are being applied in the educational field, question two asked participants to discuss other translanguaging methods that they would recommend. Accordingly, participants recommended the professional development of teachers with regard to the English language; use of other indigenous languages apart from Swahili; asking students to translate vocabulary from English to Swahili and vice versa; use of codeswitching strategies to facilitate understanding of complex contents; use of teaching aids such as pictures, diagrams, songs, and stories. Markedly, one participant said, "Where necessary, other local languages apart from Swahili should be used especially in matters or topics that are associated with cultural affairs. However, the class has to be homogenous in tribe."

While most of the participants proposed a variety of translanguaging strategies, the minority (38%) maintained that the monolingual approach (EOP) should not be replaced by any other method. For example, participant K said, "The strategy I recommend to the English teacher is to use only English language when they are teaching, this is because it led to the higher performance."

Conclusion

The central focus of this chapter was to present the findings of the survey about the effectiveness of translanguaging strategies as far as teaching EFL goes. As has been noted from the majority opinion, both Likert Scale responses and responses from essay questions affirm that English educators apply translanguaging strategies (albeit at various levels); that the strategies facilitate lesson comprehension; and that students become active and display satisfaction and less stress when their teacher uses Swahili to clarify some concepts.

On another note, most participants dismissed popular beliefs that translanguaging strategies suggest the teacher's lack of proficiency in English; that codeswitching confuses students; and that the same method impedes students' acquisition of English skills. Instead, they unanimously attributed their failure to master the English language to the EOP that has been in force for decades. Furthermore, even though participants disapproved of negative beliefs vis-à-vis translanguaging, they concurred that using EOP enables the teacher to win respect from students and acquaintances and that the same policy is associated with a high level of education. Finally, participants recommended the insertional and alternational methods as the most effective strategies of translanguaging.

Contrastingly, some participants believed that translanguaging techniques are ineffective and a reason for students' failure to master the language. They argued that EOP should be maintained because it gives students self-confidence, a sense of self-worth, and links them to the global society. Nevertheless, participants who supported the use of translanguaging strategies outnumber those who challenged the method.

Chapter 5

Data Evaluation and Interpretation

Chapter four presented a synthesis of survey responses to the central question: "What are Tanzanian educators' core beliefs and perspectives related to the effectiveness of translanguaging strategies in teaching EFL to secondary school students?" For the most part, the responses suggested that English educators in Tanzania believe that translanguaging is effective and practical and would bring about a positive outcome if the Ministry of Education officially approved the typical instructional pedagogy. That way, the research findings answered the central research question affirmatively. Accordingly, the present chapter digs into the meaning, importance, and relevance of the responses to the research question and sub-questions. Also, the chapter relates research findings with the existing literature and discusses the practical implication of the results, with particular attention to the Tanzanian context.

It is important to note that the data were interpreted from the emic and etic perspectives. Regarding the former, the PI explicated the data based on his personal experience since he was schooled under the English Only Policy. Concerning the latter, the PI took an outsider position and explained reflective ideas, thoughts, speculations, feelings, and impressions generated by research findings (American University, n.d.). The final thing to note is that the discussion in this chapter focuses on translanguaging techniques and their application, the efficacy of translanguaging strategies, students' attitudes toward translanguaging, practitioners' opinions on the English Only Policy, sociocultural beliefs vis-à-vis translanguaging, and finally, recommendations.

Translanguaging Techniques and their Application

Both sub-questions one and seven of the survey instrument are discussed jointly in this section because of their co-relation. In particular, question one asked if participants use translanguaging techniques, and if their answer was affirmative, they were required to explain the manner and the extent to which they do so. Likewise, question seven required participants to indicate the extent to which specific translanguaging techniques apply to their teaching practice. The two questions sought to ascertain from participants whether translanguaging is being practiced in the Tanzanian context—since, as noted previously, the only official language of instruction is English. As could be noted, the nature of the responses to these questions was central to the relevance of this study. If participants answered negatively, the entire course of the study would have been altered. However, a positive response was anticipated since most educators practice translanguaging informally to facilitate learning. The PI knew this from his schooling experience under the English Only Policy (EOP). Accordingly, participants affirmed the use of translanguaging in their teaching careers. For instance, 7 out of 15 participants said they occasionally, 4 seldom, 2 always, and 1 frequently use translanguaging. The implication of the participants who selected "Occasionally" is that teachers do not allow Swahili to dominate instruction lest it undermine the fundamental purpose of helping students acquire English skills. This supports Pei-shi (2012) who, while investigating if L1 is necessary for the English learning process, concluded that students indicate a desire to have a teacher use L1 for an average of 20% of the lesson time.

Although most participants claimed that they never allow students to alternate between languages when responding to questions during the lesson, the data obtained from research sub-question 7 showed that almost 90% of teachers give students the liberty to use the language of their choice during group discussions. Certainly, by not allowing students to translanguage during the lesson, teachers intend to control the use of Swahili.

On the other hand, participants said "No" when asked whether principals allow teachers to use translanguaging strategies. This answer was anticipated. Since the official policy is English-only, one would not expect school principals to formally permit translanguaging techniques. However, as can be judged from research findings, principals turn a deaf ear and a blind eye to the informal use of translanguaging techniques. In effect, principals' indifferent attitude to the violation of the EOP turns out to be necessary for students' success, since, as one participant remarked, "[Without translanguaging] the performance would go down because some students have a low command of the English language. I have experienced cases where a student asks the explanation to be repeated in Swahili having not understood when English was purely used."

Also, from survey results, it was made clear that the insertional strategy (that is, the practice of incorporating a few Swahili words in a predominantly English speech) is the most applied. Both the results of questions 1 and 7 affirm the said practice. For instance, in question 1, most participants said they occasionally use the strategy, and in question 7 they said sometimes they incorporate a few Swahili words in a predominantly English speech.

On the other hand, findings suggest that the alternational method (delivering part of the speech in English and part of it in Swahili) is not widely applied since only 43.7% of participants said they sometimes use the technique while another 43.7% said they never use it. It appears that the alternational method is used only when a student asks for clarification of particular concepts to be given in Swahili after failing to understand them in English. This idea allows students an opportunity to hone their cognitive skills in both languages, and it aligns with Garcia and Kano (2014), who maintained that when students are allowed to express themselves in L1, they develop their thinking in that same language, and when the development of that thinking is not conditioned to occur in L2, they can write well in L2 once they develop proficiency in it. Another key point is that intersentential translanguaging occurs naturally and frequently, and it helps students draw from across their existing language skills rather than restricting themselves within monolingual instructional assumptions (Hornberger & Link, 2012).

However, there were a few negative remarks about translanguaging, and it is possible that these might have come from participants who were schooled under the English Medium system from kindergarten through high school. Experience shows that students who are exposed to English from a young age do not usually find any problem with the EOP since they have an opportunity to experience what Celce-Murcia, Brinton, and Snow (2014) called *early total immersion program* in which most or all academic instruction—beginning in kindergarten or grade one—is exclusively conducted in English. This idea was affirmed by one participant who said, "It was easy for me to learn and understand because I had a good basis of the English language that I had acquired in my lower levels of schooling." According to Denham and Lobeck (2018), these students have greater chances of acquiring proficiency in L2 and tend to have increased mental capabilities, creativity, and a higher order of thinking skills. However, private schools that provide typical educational environments are overly expensive, and only a few affluent families can afford to send their children there.

The Efficacy of Translanguaging Strategies

One of the important results of this study was that participants affirmed the effectiveness of translanguaging strategies. In fact, the highest number of participants (8 out of 15) responded in agreement that translanguaging strategies facilitate lesson comprehension in the Tanzanian context. Equally significant was participants' agreement that translanguaging creates a carefree atmosphere and decreases anxiety during the lesson. These findings support Auerbach's (1993) scholarly work, which recorded that translanguaging between L1 and L2 reduces practical barriers to English acquisition, allows for more rapid progress in English acquisition, and empowers students with a limited background of literacy and schooling. Auerbach's (1993) contention aligns with a comment from one of the participants who said, "Translanguaging instructional strategies are very effective as they bring in the sense of inclusiveness."

The phrase "sense of inclusiveness" connotes the approach of accommodating both students of a limited background of literacy and those fluent in English.

Furthermore, the responses cited above reiterate the idea that translanguaging strategies are widely applied in the Tanzanian educational context even though the current educational policy is English-only. The comment given by participant G needs a special mention in this regard. She said, "Effectiveness of translanguaging depends on the class level whereby its [sic] most effective in lower levels of education especially from form one and two but from form three, single language does not hinder learning process to a greater extent." G's argument sounds reasonable since most form one (grade 7) students face linguistic challenges as they transition from Swahili as their medium of instruction in primary schools to English in secondary schools.

Conversely, G proposed a "single language use" (monolingualism) as students advance to higher levels of secondary education. However, this suggestion may not be appropriate since it will likely lead us back to the EOP that we are trying to abandon. Also, the use of what G calls "single language" would deprive students of an opportunity to draw from their existing language resources and restrict them within monolingual instructional assumptions (Hornberger & Link, 2012).

Another surprising finding of this study was that participants differed on the statement, "Rather than insisting on the monolingual (English-only) policy, the Ministry of Education should allow teachers to use both English and Swahili as official languages of instruction." While approximately 50% of participants agreed with the statement, another 50% disagreed. The implication is that while most participants acknowledged the effectiveness of translanguaging strategies in the previous question, the same participants showed a reluctant attitude toward authorizing translanguaging as an official policy of instruction. These results suggest that participants might have either misinterpreted the question or were concerned about making a statement that would otherwise contradict the existing EOP. Another possible concern is that if both languages (Swahili and English) were approved, Swahili would dominate classroom instruction and eventually undermine students' competence in English. However, this problem could be avoided if the Ministry of Education developed a curriculum that provides clear guidance on applying translanguaging strategies. In any case, there is a need to educate teachers and students about the importance of replacing the monolingual policy with translanguaging.

Students' Attitude to Translanguaging

To avoid imposing on students a teaching method that would otherwise be at odds with their preferred learning style, sub-question three sought to determine students' attitude on translanguaging. Accordingly, the question stated: "How do your students respond to the incorporation of Swahili in the EFL lesson?" About 85% of participants said their students *always* or *sometimes* understand the lesson better when the teacher explains certain concepts in Swahili. Notably, these responses reflect the scenario encountered by a Saudi Ph.D. student who, after graduating in a linguistic program in the U.S, returned to teach under the EOP in her country, only to realize that students were resistant to the policy. However, after translanguaging between Arabic and English, she recorded that the results were immediate: Students were responsive and actively engaged (Brutt-Groffler, 2017).

Likewise, the highest percentage of participants indicated that students become more active in class and display satisfaction and less stress when the teacher uses Swahili to clarify the meaning of words and phrases. These attitudes seem to suggest that students have positive thinking toward translanguaging, are optimistic about the pedagogical method, and expect a good outcome if the said method was officially authorized. Studies conducted by Pei-shi (2012) and Ahmad and Jusoff (2009) support this idea. They found out that translanguaging helps students better comprehend a lesson, understand different concepts they encounter in learning, understand new vocabulary, recognize complex concepts, and know how to use grammar rules appropriately. These results also suggest that Tanzanian students can embrace translanguaging strategies with a ready will and enthusiasm.

To find out whether translanguaging can be applied beyond the English class, one of the essay questions asked whether participants would recommend the method to other educators in the multilingual classrooms. Participants' responses proved that students encounter difficulties comprehending other lessons much as they do in the English class. Therefore, they indicated that using translanguaging strategies in lessons other than English would help students break through linguistic barriers and master the lessons. This idea seems to advocate the proposal that translanguaging strategies should be extended to other subject areas in order for educational efforts in Tanzania to bring forth good results.

In fact, participants' opinions on this question need to be considered since most students in a multilingual classroom remain tongue-tied during the lesson not because they do not have the correct answers or right ideas to contribute but because lack of competence and fluency in English denies them the freedom of expression. This reality was pointed out by one participant who said, "Denying learners the translanguaging platform in their course of learning makes some of them fail to perform in their studies as they can't express what they know or can do. Some have failed in exams not because they know little or nothing of what they were taught but because they can't express what they know in English." Consequently, a teacher may end up misjudging a student as dull or low achieving. Also, these observations align with Turkan and Liu's (2012) study, which concluded that if students do not have the necessary skills in the language of instruction, they often have a problem obtaining access to the lesson content. As a result, they are precluded from demonstrating the full repertoire of the content knowledge they have. In consequence, they lack motivation, interest, and knowledge development.

Additionally, these results confirm Al-Nofaie's (2010) study, which reported that students favored the use of Arabic in an EFL class and expressed the desire to practice the foreign language. For instance, "They [students] did not ignore the comfort that Arabic can create, especially when used for a certain purpose" (p. 78). On the contrary, these opinions suggest that denying teachers the opportunity to use translanguaging strategies precipitates lesson comprehension and arouses among students the attitude of dislike toward the lesson.

Another outstanding remark from participants was on the approach to the use of translanguaging strategies to improve students' attitudes toward the lesson. They insisted on constantly reminding students of the universality of the English language and that they need to be fluent in it to connect with the global society. Precisely, one participant mentioned that "I tell my students that when I use Swahili, it is because I couldn't find the better means to clarify what I had to clarify in English." This remark means that some teachers incorporate Swahili in an English lesson only when there is a dire need. While this motive sounds legitimate, it nevertheless overlooks another important aspect of translanguaging: sustaining students' linguistic pluralism and all the benefits it entails.

Aside from the pro-translanguaging remarks discussed above, a small number of participants commented negatively concerning students' attitudes to translanguaging. As an illustration, one participant asserted that "I would not invite this again in teaching, because by my experience, students enjoys [sic] a good flow of language." The phrase "a good flow of language" implies that most students admire and appreciate teachers who speak English fluently without appealing to translanguaging. While this approach can motivate students to learn English, it can, at the same time, exclude them from lesson comprehension.

As can be judged from most of the responses to this question, Tanzanian students have a positive attitude toward translanguaging strategies. The overall implication is that if the translanguaging pedagogical methods were to be introduced into the educational system, students would readily accept it, and indeed, it would be in accord with the learner-centered ideology (Schiro, 2013).

Practitioners' Opinion on the EOP

The survey data regarding teachers' perspectives on the EOP in Tanzania highlight three significant inferences: a) Switching from one language to another does not suggest the teacher's lack of proficiency in English, b) alternating from one language to another neither confuses students nor does it impede their acquisition of English skills, and c) using English only during instruction provides more exposure to English and more chances of acquiring the language. In particular, research findings contradict a widespread belief that those who alternate between languages during a conversation do not know either language very well. Instead, research findings confirm Denham and Lobeck's (2018) study, which established that translanguaging alludes to a speaker's great deal of grammatical and conversational expertise in two languages. Also, when a teacher uses a Swahili word or phrase to clarify an English concept, it is because that word or phrase has a meaning the English word doesn't. Thus, if a teacher remembers a word or phrase in Swahili, she doesn't need to search for close equivalents in English—she may effortlessly translanguage to clarify the concept.

Also, research findings do not fit the belief that translanguaging confuses students or interferes with convenient learning. Instead, the findings align with and even develop further the existing literature. For example, as discussed in *Chapter 2: Literature Review*, the existing literature maintains that using the EOP interferes with learning when it hinders thorough comprehension, prevents full participation, and creates a psychological blockage (Jan & Young, 2010). That is to say, research discredited the effectiveness of the EOP. Furthermore, while affirming the weakness of the EOP, research findings confirmed that translanguaging facilitates comprehension and promotes students' attitudes to the lesson. By the same token, the results support Mile's (2004) contention that many English teachers in Tanzania are non-native speakers. Therefore, the EOP may, and certainly does, impede their ability to communicate efficiently with students and consequently undermines their teaching ability.

Additionally, the results seem to align with the hypothesis that the EOP provides learners with more exposure to the foreign language and adequate chances of practicing it. However, as we noted earlier, this hypothesis focuses on acquiring English skills at the expense of skills in other subject areas. It should be noted that English is learned not only to facilitate communication but also to enhance comprehension of lessons other than English.

Furthermore, responses to this section provide supplemental evidence concerning teachers' informal application of translanguaging strategies. The graphic example of this phenomenon can be found in participant D's response, who reported having been educated under the EOP but admitted that teachers used Swahili and sometimes vernacular words to help students understand. Also, participants E and F reported similar results and added that when they adhered to the EOP, students' response was minimal and consequently had no choice but to occasionally resort to code-meshing to facilitate lesson comprehension. These results suggest that any endeavor to educate children in a multilingual society like Tanzania cannot succeed without allowing teachers and students to use their available language resources to their potential.

In general, participants' opinions on the EOP were mainly negative. They described it as a policy that undermines the strength of the national language (Swahili), causes tension and a stressful atmosphere during the lesson, and creates fear and a lack of confidence, especially among students who hail from public primary schools.

Sociocultural Beliefs vis-à-vis Translanguaging

In item one of sub-question five, participants elucidated their beliefs as well as those of the society regarding the phenomenon of translanguaging. Most of these responses indicated that an educator's fluency in English commands respect and admiration of students and acquaintances. Similar results were recorded in item two of the same question in which participants unanimously agreed that fluency in English is associated with a high level of education. Despite the agreement between research findings and popular beliefs, one cannot ignore the fact that upholding the same beliefs and sidelining translanguaging practices deprives students of manifold cultural benefits. As discussed previously, when students are encouraged to switch between languages, they are empowered with language creativity in speech and become more successful in learning other languages (Vladmirovna, Sergreevna, & Vladislavovna, 2020). On the other hand, when teachers choose to adhere to the EOP and speak English fluently to inspire students, they do not benefit students in any practical way other than showcasing their linguistic expertise and compounding students' poor comprehension of the lesson.

On another note, the results contradicted the belief that insisting on the EOP is an attempt to adapt students to the western world and alienate them from their own people and culture. The highest percentage of participants disagreed with the belief. This suggests Tanzanians understand that English is a global *lingua franca* and not just the language of western countries. Therefore, adhering to the EOP is not an attempt to derogate their cultural values but to connect to the rest of the world because English is priced in various domains such as technology, international business, diplomacy, etc. This idea was backed up by Petzell (2012), who noted that English and Swahili have separate roles in society, so it is not contradictory to think highly of both languages since they have different domains.

Furthermore, it was interesting to note that the responses to essay-type questions built on the existing literature. Most of the participants argued that translanguaging should be allowed in secondary schools for the sake of securing Tanzanians' sense of identity, social belonging, and self-worth. They also explained that since most Tanzanians value both Swahili and English languages, translanguaging will not threaten national culture but promote it. These results contribute to the ideas of Bwenge (2012), who reasoned that since English is learned in a predominantly Swahili environment—with students interacting on a daily basis with families, playmates, local business, etc., in Swahili—the effective learning of English dictates the use of translanguaging strategies between the two languages. This means that as long as students interact with other people in Swahili, translanguaging during classroom instruction could be the best way to sustain students' cultural values and social belonging.

Although some comments from participants did not synchronize with the existing literature, they provided new insights on the cultural aspect of translanguaging strategies. For instance, F argued that we should maintain the EOP because it gives students a sense of pride as well as self-worth. Conversely, G insisted that Swahili should be used at all levels of education and communication since it is the national language. On one hand, F's contention implies that we should continue embracing the EOP and stigmatizing Tanzanians' native language (Swahili), national identity, and culture. On the other hand, G's position implies that we should endorse Swahili only to safeguard Tanzania's cultural values but isolate Tanzanians from the global society. In fact, there is no convenient way of solving this dilemma other than embracing translanguaging pedagogical methods during classroom instruction.

Recommendations

A good body of literature combined with bountiful evidence from Tanzania has proven that adherence to the EOP during classroom instruction acts as a barrier to lesson comprehension, particularly for students who hail from communities where Swahili and other indigenous languages are dominant. As a solution, the author recommends that the Ministry of Education consider developing an instructional policy that would allow the use of Swahili alongside

English in order to accommodate both minority students who come from English medium schools and the majority who went to public schools where Swahili was the medium of instruction. Additionally, the Ministry of Education may need to consider adapting the insertional and alternational methods during instruction, creating opportunities for professional development of English educators, and adapting instructional methods that sustain students' cultural identity. This section provides some suggestions and policies that can be followed to achieve the goals itemized above.

Inclusivity

As noted previously, participants indicated that a few students who were schooled under the English medium private institutions from kindergarten have no problem understanding lessons when conducted exclusively in English. This perspective has always served to accentuate the confounded cultural belief *that speaking English fluently is associated with high esteem and a high level of education.* However, the same policy precipitates students' understanding especially those recruited from public primary schools where Swahili is the only medium. According to Jha (2020), the said policy leads to "silencing" the students and is the main contributor to a low level of learning outcome. Consequently, the often "silenced" students are likely to be construed as dull or slow learners. Also, research has demonstrated that the language barrier has always prevented brilliant students from demonstrating the extent of their knowledge.

To promote the atmosphere of inclusivity, respect, and social cohesion in the Tanzanian multilingual classroom, the author recommends that the application of translanguaging strategies be prioritized in the secondary school curriculum. This would ensure accommodation and inclusiveness between students of limited proficiency and those who struggle with the language.

Adapting Alternational and Insertional Methods

Based on the research findings, the translanguaging methods that work best in the Tanzanian context are alternational and insertional. To recapitulate, the alternational method refers to delivering part of the speech in English and part of it in Swahili, while the insertional method means inserting a few Swahili words in a predominantly English sentence (speech). Of the two methods, however, the alternational method would be more practical for two reasons: a) it allows both students and teachers to bring in language-specific resources (for example, explaining sayings or proverbs in Swahili that cannot be easily translated to English), thereby making a conversation easier, and b) it preserves the grammar and syntax of both languages (English and Swahili). In other words, the grammar and syntax of the languages are not adulterated through the insertion of foreign words or syllables. However, to properly apply this strategy, the teacher must be fluent in both languages because it requires the speaker to switch to the rules of syntax of the other language mid-thought or sentence, and consequently may be avoided by all but the most fluent of bilingual speakers (Zicker, 2007).

On the other hand, the insertional method can be used in circumstances where, in the course of conversation, a speaker is compelled to borrow a word or phrase from another language simply because the present language proves inadequate to explicate a particular concept. Although this strategy facilitates lesson comprehension and accommodates both students of high and limited proficiency in English, one may need to limit it to only a few instances on account of the potential danger it poses. If overused, the strategy can result in the creation of a new variety of language through word borrowing. It should be noted that the purpose of proposing translanguaging strategies is not to create a distinct type of language but to empower students with English skills, facilitate lesson comprehension, and help students sustain their native language (Swahili).

Other methods can be used to supplement insertional and alternational strategies. For instance, teachers can engage students in multilingual writing partners by allowing them to brainstorm ideas on the topic in Swahili and then write in English; have them jointly construct a piece of writing in English and then discuss, negotiate, and give suggestions in Swahili; have them read a partner's writing in English then discuss revisions and edit it in Swahili. Also, teachers can use multilingual texts or bilingual dictionaries during instruction. These techniques help students build background knowledge about Swahili text, which improves students' comprehension while reading the related text in English. Also, English-Swahili dictionaries can help students understand the most critical keywords needed to comprehend the English concepts.

Mentorship & Professional Development for English Educators

For the practical implementation of translanguaging strategies to succeed, English educators should receive training and mentorship on how and when to use the strategies. Experienced teachers who themselves have successfully applied translanguaging could be the best mentors to those who have yet to apply the method. Mentors can help explain the reasons, significance, advantages, relevance, as well as the best approach for implementing translanguaging strategies. On the other hand, inexperienced teachers can take the initiative to talk with experienced teachers in or beyond their schools, observe them teaching, and ask them to share ideas vis-à-vis the application of translanguaging strategies (Slavin, 2015). Apart from making the most of experienced and helpful mentors, schools can create induction programs to help new teachers develop translanguaging skills.

Coupled with mentorship, the Ministry of Education can organize professional development workshops on translanguaging for secondary school teachers across districts. Facilitators from regions or countries where translanguaging has been successfully implemented can be invited to assist English educators. As they meet for workshops, teachers from the same school can discuss the success and challenges of translanguaging in their field of practice.

Generally speaking, workshops, training, and seminars are less expensive and can help facilitate the implementation of translanguaging strategies far better than taking a degree program. These three (workshops, training, and seminars) are known for keeping educators updated with the latest trends, skills, and information essential for their professional growth (Slavin, 2015).

Educating Students on the Importance of Translanguaging

An adage goes: "You can bring a horse to water, but you can't make it drink; it will drink when it is ready"—and so, with people. The proverb means that students may not embrace translanguaging strategies unless they are motivated and educated about the importance of the pedagogical method. This is particularly necessary for students who were schooled under the EOP in the English medium primary schools prior to joining secondary education. As discussed previously, this category of students and educators was opposed to translanguaging and spoke highly of the EOP.

Thus, students can be instructed about the need to accept translanguaging strategies as a way of encouraging them to recruit all their linguistic resources in literacy tasks, rather than separating languages. Furthermore, they can be made to understand that translanguaging pedagogies can support them in more complex literacy practices and cognitive tasks they cannot accomplish monolingually (Lee &Handsfield, 2018). Additional information from Denham and Lobeck (2013) about how translanguaging gives students a wider range of linguistic tools at their disposal and empowers them with cognitive skills can be used to support this claim.

Additionally, students should know that by introducing translanguaging, we aim to facilitate a better understanding of class content, create a stronger home-school connection, and allow for better participation between weaker and stronger learners in the bilingual classroom (Paulsrud et al., 2017). However, as they communicate with people in real-life settings, students should consider the nature of the audience and decide where, when, and how to translanguage. To illustrate this concept, we shall use Kirkpatrick's (2007) example of *The Functions of Language and the Identity-Communication Continuum.* Let us imagine a Tanzanian businessman traveling to the U.S to talk to his counterparts there. It is likely that the major function that he will want his language to fulfill is the communicative function. He will then take care to edit out specific *Swahilism* from his speech and try to make his accent sound less Tanzanian so that his American colleague can understand what he says. Now, let us imagine that the Tanzanian's mobile phone rings and it is his son calling from their home in Tanzania. It is very likely that the identity and cultural functions of language will become more important. This means that when speaking to his son, the Tanzanian will feel free to translanguage between English and Swahili and use a far more specific vocabulary of Swahili and cultural references. Hence, students need to understand that translanguaging is meant to sustain these functions of language.

Protecting Students' Cultural Identity

Unfortunately, research findings showed that people associate fluency in English with respect and a high level of education. Consequently, the EOP is perceived as the best way to achieve these values. However, as we discussed in the data evaluation section, this sociocultural belief may be a mere illusion or at least a myth. One does not need to be fluent in English in order to be educated. In other words, fluency in English is not the measure of intelligence, nor can fluency in English be limited to education. Language also has to do with a person's identity and culture. As noted by Reynolds (2019), "Language is not only a medium of learning but also an intrinsic part of one's identity, and decisions about languages to teach and use as part of formal schooling not only directly impact educational outcomes but also create implicit messages about whether students' heritages and identities are welcome and capable of succeeding at school" (p. 6). Thus, the Ministry of Education must consider protecting students' cultural identity and not focus exclusively on helping students attain linguistic competence through the EOP. According to Bonvillain (2020), language and culture; culture and communication are intimately connected. In many ways, speakers use language to accomplish goals and express their intentions. Also, the meanings of cultural symbols and social and political dimensions can only be best described through language. In fact, words convey many kinds of cultural meanings that add to, transform, or manipulate the basic sense of utterances.

Furthermore, word choice, tone of voice, or facial expressions rely on cultural and social norms. Although some of these cultural concepts can be expressed through the English language once a speaker has acquired proficiency and communicative competence, other concepts in the Tanzanian culture cannot be appropriately translated into English. This implies that once a student delves into English learning through the EOP, s/he is likely to lose important aspects of his/her identity and culture. The best solution would be to use English side-by-side with Swahili during classroom instruction. Hence, the need for translanguaging cannot be overstated.

Chapter 6

General Conclusion

This chapter concludes the study by synthesizing the key findings and discussing the relationship between the said findings and research questions. It also reviews the study's main contribution to the educational field, the procedural limitations, as well as opportunities for future research.

Key Findings

The study's primary purpose was to explore Tanzanian educators' beliefs and perspectives on the effectiveness of translanguaging strategies in teaching English as a Foreign Language (EFL) to secondary school students. Previous studies conducted in contexts other than Tanzania had proven that translanguaging helps bilingual students self-regulate their language practices in learning, harness their diverse linguistic and cultural repertoires, and facilitate the sustenance of their native languages (Garcia & Kano, 2014; Creese & Blackledge, 2010; Hornberger & Link, 2012). Also, the same studies maintained that translanguaging gives multilingual students a more comprehensive range of linguistic tools at their disposal, equips them with superior communicative sensitivity, and empowers them with cognitive skills as opposed to their monolingual counterparts (Denham & Lobeck, 2018). However, these facts were yet to be authenticated in the Tanzania context since no previous research had explored the matter with a specific focus on the country. Accordingly, the study was motivated by the central question: "What are Tanzanian educators' core beliefs and perspectives related to the effectiveness of translanguaging strategies in teaching EFL to secondary school students?"

For the most part, research findings suggested that translanguaging strategies facilitate lesson comprehension, create a carefree atmosphere, decrease anxiety during the lesson, and empower students with limited backgrounds of literacy and learning. Also, survey results indicated that most students in Tanzania become more active in class and display satisfaction and less stress when the teacher switches between English and Swahili to clarify the meaning of words and phrases. Conversely, results evidenced that banning the application of translanguaging strategies in the Tanzania multilingual classroom precludes students from demonstrating the entire repertoire of the content knowledge they have and deprives them of motivation, interest, and knowledge development.

Contribution to the Field of Education

As noted earlier, no previous study had addressed the need and relevance of translanguaging strategies in the Tanzanian context. Educational policymakers in Tanzania still believe that the use of translanguaging strategies suggests the teacher's lack of proficiency in English, confuses students and impedes their acquisition of English skills. Nevertheless, the research findings have proven just the opposite. The effectiveness of translanguaging strategies that has been brought to the fore—thanks to the positive survey results—

will most undoubtedly prompt education policymakers to adapt the said strategies.

To reach a wider audience and encourage change, especially among education policymakers in Tanzania, the results of this study have been published in a book form both as a hard copy and electronically. The hope is that once adapted, translanguaging strategies will help students cherish their multilingual heritage and sustain their cultural identity—let alone enhance their lesson comprehension and linguistic development.

Limitations and Shortcomings

As specified previously in *Chapter 3: Methodology*, the study relied exclusively on an online survey for data collection. A multi-method research approach such as participant observation and interviews would have created a more in-depth picture of the research problem and, consequently, enhanced validity. However, the factors of distance and poor technology in the research context compounded the possibility of data triangulation. For the same reasons of distance and poor technology, the final report of the collected data was not taken back to participants to determine whether they felt that the findings were accurate. This procedure, also known as member checking, would have furthered the validity of the findings.

Additionally, the sample size that was designated for the research appears to be too small to reflect the target population and validate the generalization of conclusions. Large sample size required adequate funding and, unfortunately, this study was unfunded. The purpose of highlighting these shortcomings is not to undermine the credibility of this study but to show that we are aware of the limitations of the research design that was espoused.

Opportunities for Future Research

This study can be duplicated using multiple and more sophisticated methods of data collection in order to compare the data for convergence, complementarity, and divergence—hence, triangulation (Nightingale, 2020). This approach would help ensure that different methods or observers of the same phenomenon produce the same results and therefore, enhance the accuracy of the findings. Furthermore, future research can undertake a similar study using a large sample size. For instance, instead of using samples from the three administrative regions (Kagera, Mwanza, and Dar es Salaam), a researcher can recruit participants from at least thirteen regions across the country (since Tanzania has a total of 27 administrative regions) in order to achieve a representative picture of the whole population.

All things considered, this study has scored its goal of attesting to the effectiveness of translanguaging strategies and appealing to the educational policymakers in Tanzania to consider espousing the said approach as a viable alternative for teaching English instead of exclusively relying on the monolingual policy.

References

Abdulaziz-Mkilifi, M. (1972). Triglossia and Swahili-English bilingualism in Tanzania. *Language in Society*, 1(2), 197-213. Retrieved from https://www.jstor.org/stable/4166684?seq=1#metadata_info_tab_contents

Ahmad, B. H. & Jusoff, K. (2009). Teachers' code-switching in classroom instructions for low English proficient learners. *English Language Teaching*, 2(2), 49-55. Retrieved from https://files.eric.ed.gov/fulltext/EJ1082375.pdf

Al-Nofaie, H. (2010). Attitudes of teachers and students towards using Arabic in EFL classrooms in Saudi public schools: A case study. *Novitas-ROYAL (Research on Youth and Language)*, 4(1), pp. 64-95. Retrieved from http://www.novitasroyal.org/Vol_4_1/al-nofaie.pdf

Al Tale, M. & Alqahtani, F. A. (2012). Codeswitching versus target-language only for English as a foreign language: Saudi students' perception. *English Language Teaching*, 13(9), 18-29. doi:10.5539/elt.v13n9p18

American Psychological Association (APA). (2010). *Publication manual of the American psychological association*. Washington, DC: American Psychological Association.

American University. (n.d.). Qualitative methods in monitoring and evaluation: The emic and the etic: Their importance to qualitative evaluators. Retrieved from https://programs.online.american.edu/msme/masters-in-measurement-and-evaluation/resources/emic-and-etic

Auerbach, E. R. (1993). Reexamining English only in the ESL classroom. *TESOL Quarterly*, 27(1), 1-18. Retrieved from https://www.jstor.org/stable/3586949

Blommaert, J. (2014). *State ideology and language in Tanzania*. Edinburg: Edinburg University Press. Retrieved from https://www.researchgate.net/publication/272183753_State _Ideology_and_Language_in_Tanzania_Second_and_Revised_Edition

Bonvillain, N. (2020). *Language, culture, and communication: The meaning of messages*, 8th ed. New York, NY: Rowman and Littlefield.

Brutt-Griffler, K. (2017). English in the multilingual classroom: Implications for research, policy, and practice. *PSV Research Review*, 1(3), 216-228. Retrieved from https://www.emerald.com/ insight/content/doi/10.1108/PRR-10-2017-0042/full/html/

Burden, P. (2000). The use of students' mother tongue in monolingual English conversation classes at Japanese universities. *The Language Teacher*, 24(6), 5-10.

Bwenge, C. (2012). English in Tanzania: A linguistic cultural perspective. *International Journal of Language, Translation, and Intercultural Communication*, 1, 1-16. Retrieved from https://ejournals.epublishing.ekt.gr/index.php/latic/article/ view/2724/2499

Celce-Murcia, M., Brinton, D. M., & Snow M. A. (Eds.). (2014). *Teaching English as a second or foreign language* (4th ed.). Boston, MA: Heinle Cengage Learning.

Celic, C. & Seltzer, K. (2013). *Translanguaging: A cuny-nysieb guide for educators*. New York, NY: Cuny-Nysieb. Retrieved from

https://www.cuny-nysieb.org/wp-content/uploads/2016/04/
Translanguaging-Guide-March-2013.pdf

Cochran-Smith, M. & Lytle, L. S. (2009). *Inquiry as stance: Practitioner research for the next generation.* New York, NY: Teachers College Press.

Cenoz, J., & Gorter, D. (2011). Focus on multilingualism: A study of trilingual writing. *The Modern Language Journal,* 95, 356–369. doi:10.1111/ j.1540-4781.2011.01206.x

Creese, A. & Blackledge, A. (2010). Translanguaging in the bilingual classroom: A pedagogy for learning and teaching? *The Modern Language Journal,* 94(1), 103-115. Retrieved from https://doi.org/10.1111/j.1540-4781.2009.00986.x

_____ *Multilingualism: A critical perspective.* London: Bloomsbury Publishing. Retrieved from https://www.bloomsbury.com/us/multilingualism-9780826492098/

Creswell, J. W., & Creswell, J. D. (2018*). Research design: Qualitative, quantitative, and mixed methods approaches,* (5th ed.). Los Angeles, CA: Sage Publications, Inc.

Cummins, J. (2007). Rethinking monolingual instructional strategies in multilingual classrooms. Retrieved from https://researchgate.net/publication/228368309_Rethinking_Monolingual_Instructional_Strategies_in_Multilingual_Classrooms

Dana, N. F., & Yendol-Hoppey, D. (2014). *The reflective educator's guide to classroom research: Learning to teach and teaching to learn* (3rd ed.). California, CA: Corwin, A Sage Company.

Denham, K. & Lobeck, A. (2013). *Linguistics for everyone: An introduction* (2nd ed.). Boston, MA: Wadsworth, Cengage Learning.

Ekawati, S. M., & Setyarini, M. C. E. (2014). Students' attitude to-
    ward monolingual approach in   English classes at SMA LAB
    Salatiga. Retrieved from file:///C:/Users/Thomas/OneDrive/
    Desktop/Murray%20SU/J01421.pdf

Ferguson, G. (2003). Classroom code-switching in post-colonial
    contexts: Functions, attitudes and policies. *African and Applied
    Linguistics*, 16(1), 1-15. DOI: 10.1075/aila.16.05fer

Garcia, O. & Kano, N. (2014). Translanguaging as process and ped-
    agogy: Developing the English writing of Japanese students in
    the US. In Conteh, J. & Meier, G. (Eds.), *The multilingual turn
    in languages education: Opportunities and challenges* (pp. 258-
    277). London, UK: Multilingual Matters.

García, O., & Leiva, C. (2014). Theorizing and enacting translan-
    guaging for social justice. In Blackledge, A., & Creese, A. (Eds.),
    Heteroglossia as practice and pedagogy (pp. 199–216). Dor-
    drecht, Netherlands: Springer.

Heller, M. (1988). *Codeswitching: Anthropological and sociolinguis-
    tic perspectives*. Berlin: Mouton de Gruyter.

Hoang, N. T., Jang, S. H., & Yang, Y. (2010, December). *English-
    only classrooms: Ideology versus reality*. Paper presented at the
    AARE Annual Conference Melboume. Retrieved from
    https://www.aare.edu.au/data/publications/2010/1755Ho-
    angJangYang.pdf

Hornberger, N. H. & Link, H. (2012). Translanguaging and trans-
    national literacies in multilingual classrooms: A biliteracy lens.
    International Journal of Bilingual Education and Bilingualism,
    15(3), 261-278. Retrieved from https://www.tandfonline.com/
    doi/full/10.1080/13670050.2012.658016

Iwai, Y. (2011). The Effects of Metacognitive Reading Strategies: Pedagogical Implications for EFL/ESL Teachers. *The Reading Matrix*, 11(2), 150-159. Retrieved from https://readingmatrix.com/articles/april_2011/iwai.pdf

Jha, J. (2021). Public policy dilemma of choosing the medium of instruction for school education: A case study for questioning fallacies and connecting objectives. *Journal of Asian Development Research*, 1-14. Retrieved from https://journals.sagepub.com/doi/full/10.1177/2633190X211034697

Kirkpatric, A. (2007). *World Englishes: Implications for international communication and English language teaching.* London: Cambridge University Press.

Krashen, S. (1985). *The input hypothesis: Issues and implications.* New York, NY: Longman.

Lee, A. Y. & Handsfield, L. J. (2018). Code-meshing and writing instruction in multilingual classrooms. *International Literacy Association*, 72(2), 159-168. Retrieved from https://www.una.edu/education/educator-preparation/praxis-resources/Code%20Meshing%20and%20Writing%20Instruction%20in%20Multi-Lingual%20Classrooms.pdf

Lewis, G., Jones, B., & Baker, C. (2012). Translanguaging: Origins and development from school to street and beyond. *Educational Research and Evaluation*, 18(7), 641–654. doi:10.1080/13803611.2012.718488

Mehta, V. (2021). English is not a measure of intelligence. *Slice of Life.* Retrieved from https://thewanderingvegetable.com/english-is-not-a-measure-of-intelligence/

Michael-Luna, S., & Canagarajah, A. S. (2007). Multilingual academic literacies: Pedagogical foundations of code meshing in primary and higher education. *Journal of Applied Linguistics*, 4(1), 55-77. doi: 10.1558/japl.v4i1.55

Miles, R. (2004). *Evaluating the use if L1 in the English language classroom* (Doctoral dissertation, the School of Humanities, University of Birmingham). Retrieved from www.cels.bham.ac.uk/resources/essays/Milesdiss.pdf

Nakayama, T. K. & Halualani, R. T. (2010). (Eds.). *Handbook of critical intercultural communication*. Malden, MA: Blackwell Publishing Ltd. Retrieved from https://books.google.com/books?hl=en&lr=&id=KSohvQwAdnYC&oi=fnd&pg=PA1&dq=Handbook+of+critical+international+communication.+Malden&ots=sAF67FbFKT&sig=MtxbVQZFXR_za5JUHthw-9xsL1E#v=onepage&q=Handbook%20of%20critical%20international%20communication.%20Malden&f=false

Ngonyani, D. (n.d.). The Failure of Language Policy in Tanzanian Schools. Retrieved from http://www.socialstudies.org/sites/default/files/publications/se/6107/610708.html

Nightingale, A. J. (2020). Triangulation. In International Encyclopedia of Human Geography, 2nd ed. Retrieved from https://sciencedirect.com/topics/social-sciences/triangulation#:~:text=Triangulation%20is%20a%20technique%20to,of%20understanding%20a%20research%20problem.

Nilep, C. (2006). Code-switching in sociocultural linguistics. *Colorado Research in Linguistics*, 19, 1-22. doi: https://doi.org/10.25810/hnq4-jv62

Pachler, N., & Field, K. (2001). *Learning to Teach Modern Foreign Languages in the Secondary School.* London: Routledge.

Pardede, P. (2013). *Evaluation of use of MT in EFL classes of secondary schools in Jadetabek: Students and teachers' perception* (Research Proposal, Universitas Kristen Indonesia, Jakarta). Retrieved from www.scribd.com/;137890893/Proposal-Evaluation-MT-in-EFL-Class

Paulsrud, B., Rosén, J., Straszer, B., & Wedin, Å. (2017). *New perspectives on translanguaging and education* (Vol. 108). Bristol: Multilingual Matters. https://scholar.google.com/scholar_lookup?hl=en-US&publication_year=2017&author=B.+Paulsrud&author=J.+Ros%C3%A9n&author=B.+Straszer&author=%C3%85+Wedin&title=New+perspectives+on+translanguaging+and+education

Pei-shi, W. (2012). Code-switching as a strategy used in an EFL classroom in Taiwan. *US- China Foreign Language,* 10(10), 1669-1675. Retrieved from 2012.10_US- China_Foreign_Language-with-cover-page

Petzell, M. (2012). The linguistic situation in Tanzania. *Moderna Sprak,* 136-144. Retrieved from https://ojs.ub.gu.se/ojs/index.php/modernasprak/article/viewFile/1187/1026

Piasecka, K. (1988). The bilingual teacher in the ESL classroom. In Nicholls, S. & Hoadley-Maidment, E. (Eds.), *Current Issues in teaching English as a second language to adults* (pp. 97-103). London: Edward Arnold.

Piotrowski, A., & White, S. (2016). Flipped learning and TPACK construction in English education. *International Journal of Technology in Teaching and Learning,* (12(1), 33-46.

Poza, L. (2017). Translanguaging: Definitions, implications, and further need in burgeoning inquiry. *Berkeley Review of Education*, 6(2), 102-128. Retrieved from https://files.eric.ed.gov/fulltext/EJ1169828.pdf

Roy-Campbell, Z. M. (2019) The politics of education in Tanzania: From colonialism to liberalization. In Campbell, H. & Stein, H. (Eds.), *The IMF and Tanzania: Southern African political economy series trust* (pp.147-170). Harare: Taylor and Francis.

Schiro, M. S. (2013). *Curriculum theory: Conflicting visions and enduring concerns*, 2nd ed. Los Angeles, CA: Sage Publications, Inc.

Si, P. (2019). A study of the differences between EFL and ESL for English classroom teaching in China. *IRS International Journal of Education and Multidisciplinary Studies*, 15(1), 32-35. doi: http://dx.doi.org/10.21013/jems.v15.n1.p4

Slavin, R. E. (2015). *Educational psychology: Theory and practice, custom edition for Liberty University*. New York, NY: Pearson Education, Inc.

Statistica. (2020). Number of public and secondary schools in Tanzania from 2016 to 2020. Retrieved from https://www.statista.com/statistics/1280851/number-of-secondary-schools-in-tanzania-by-ownership/

Tien, C & Liu, K. (2006). Code-switching in two EFL classes in Taiwan. In Hashim, A. & Hassan, N. (Eds), *English in Southeast Asia: prospects, perspectives, and possibilities*. Kuala Lumpur: University Malaya Press.

Turkan, S., & Liu, O. L. (2012). Differential performance by English language learners on an inquiry-based science assessment.

International Journal of Science Education, 34(15), 2343–2369. doi: 10.1080/09500693.2012.705046

Van Lier, L. (2008). The ecology of language learning and sociocultural theory. In Creese, A., Martin, P., & Hornberger (Eds.), *Encyclopedia of language and education* (2nd ed., vol. 9, pp. 53-65). Boson, MA: Springer Science and Business Media.

Vladimirovna, T. E., Sergreevna,M. E., and Vladislavovna, A. A. (2020). Cultural impact of code-switching on modern bilingualism. *International Journal of Science Education*. doi: 10.1080/09500693.2012.705046

Williams, C. (2002). Extending bilingualism in the education system. *Education and Lifelong Learning Committee (ELL Report No. 06–2)*. Retrieved from http://www.assemblywales.org/3c91c7af00023d820000595000000000.pdf

Wibowo, A. I., Yuniasih, I., & Nelfianti, F. (2017). Analysis of types codeswitching and codemixing by the sixth president of the republic Indonesia's speech at the national of independence day. *Progressive*, 12(1), 13-22. Retrieved from https://media.neliti.com/media/publications/227310-analysis-of-types-code-switching-and-cod-1287515d.pdf

World Bank (1988). Education in Sub-Saharan Africa: policies for adjustment, revitalization, and expansion. *International Bank for Reconstruction and Development*, pp. 185.

World Population prospects. (2019). Tanzania population. Retrieved from https://worldpopulationreview.com/countries/tanzania-population

Worthy, L. D. (n.d.). Codeswitching. *Culture and Psychology.* Re-
    trieved from https://open.maricopa.edu/culturepsychology/
    chapter/code-switching/

Ziker, K.N. (2007). Intrasentential vs. intersentential code switch-
    ing in early and late bilinguals (Master's Thesis, Brigham Yong
    University, Provo, Utah). Retrieved from https://scholarsar-
    chive.byu.edu/cgi/viewcontent.cgi?article=1926&context=etd

Appendix

School Systems—Tanzanian Vs American

Tanzanian			American		
Phase	Standard/From	Age of Student	Age of Student	Grade Level	Phase
Pre-Primary School	Nursery	4-5	5-6	Kindergarten	Elementary School
Primary School	Standard 1	5-6	6-7	Grade 1	Elementary School
	Standard 2	6-7	7-8	Grade 2	
	Standard 3	7-8	8-9	Grade 3	
	Standard 4	8-9	9-10	Grade 4	
	Standard 5	9-10	10-11	Grade 5	
	Standard 6	10-11	11-12	Grade 6	Middle School
	Standard 7	11-12	No Equivalent		
Ordinary Secondary School (Ordinary Level)	Form 1	12-13	12-13	Grade 7	
	Form 2	13-14	13-14	Grade 8	
	Form 3	14-15	14-15	Grade 9	High School
	Form 4	15-16	15-16	Grade 10	
Advanced Secondary School (Advanced Level)	Form 5	16-17	16-17	Grade 11	High School
	Form 6	17-18	17-18	Grade 12	
Higher Education	At least 3 Years	18 and above	18 and above	At least 4 years	College Education